N
7350   Macadam, Joseph P.
M22   Japanese arts and the tea
           ceremony

94022

Japanese Arts and
the Tea Ceremony

Volume 15
THE HEIBONSHA SURVEY OF JAPANESE ART

For a list of the entire series see end of book

CONSULTING EDITORS

Katsuichiro Kamei, *art critic*
Seiichiro Takahashi, *Chairman, Japan Art Academy*
Ichimatsu Tanaka, *Chairman, Cultural Properties Protection Commission*

Japanese Arts and the Tea Ceremony

by TATSUSABURO HAYASHIYA
MASAO NAKAMURA
and SEIZO HAYASHIYA

translated and adapted by
Joseph P. Macadam

New York · WEATHERHILL/HEIBONSHA · Tokyo

This book was originally published in Japanese by Heibonsha under the title *Cha no Bijutsu* in the Nihon no Bijutsu series.

First English Edition, 1974
Second Printing, 1980

Jointly published by John Weatherhill, Inc., of New York and Tokyo, with editorial offices at 7–6–13 Roppongi, Minato-ku, Tokyo 106, and Heibonsha, Tokyo. Copyright © 1964, 1974, by Heibonsha; all rights reserved. Printed in Japan.

LCC Card No. 74–76780   *ISBN 0–8348–1025–5*

Contents

Japanese Arts and
the Tea Ceremony

CHAPTER ONE

Origins of the Tea Ceremony

TEA DRINKING HAS a long history in Japan. Even as early as the time when the priest Saicho (or Dengyo Daishi; 764–822) was propagating the tenets of Tendai Buddhism, the cult of tea had already flowered at the Heian-period (794–1185) imperial court. Tea drinking in that age is described in two anthologies of poetry in Chinese compiled by rescript of Emperor Saga (786–842; r. 809–823) in the early Heian period: the *Ryoun Shu*, the first anthology of its kind in Japan, and the *Bunka Shurei Shu* (Collection of Literary Graces). It appears to have been a pastime enjoyed by noblemen as they placidly dangled fishing lines in the waters of the pond in the spacious garden surrounding a courtier's residence and listened to the strains of koto music from within.

The *Anjo-ji Garan Engi Ruki Shizai Cho*, written in 867 and comprising the history of the Anjo-ji temple in Kyoto and an inventory of its properties, mentions the use of high-quality porcelain pots and porcelain bowls as tea utensils and lists nineteen "tea benches" among cloister articles. The tea used at the time was called "brick tea." It was made by pounding the tea leaves into a paste and molding the paste into shapes resembling dumplings, which were then brewed and finally seasoned if necessary. The people who gathered for the meeting savored this drink as they sat on folding stools prepared for the purpose. Sources like the poems contained in the anthologies mentioned above reveal that koto music almost invariably accompanied such occasions. Hence the mood characteristic of the tea drinking of Heian times would appear to have been comparable to that of the modern coffee shop provided with the sounds of background music. A poem of the time renders it thus: "The site of tranquil pleasure; the court is filled with the aroma of tea." Without doubt the court at this time deserved to be called a world of "tranquil pleasure."

It was during the Kamakura period (1185–1336) that the priest Eisai (also called Yosai; 1141–1215), who is well known for introducing the Rinzai teachings of Zen Buddhism from China, finally brought in the use of powdered green tea (*matcha*). Originally esteemed as a stimulant, used mainly to prevent the monks from falling asleep during meditation, by the early fourteenth century it had come increasingly into demand for its taste and soon emerged from its first stage of confinement in the Zen monasteries, whence it spread to samurai society and even to the rural communities. This method of drinking tea took the form of what came to be known as "tea gatherings" (*cha yoriai*), which offered a striking contrast to the quiet pleasure enjoyed by the Heian-period nobility. The tea gatherings consisted of tea contests in which the

1. *Kinkaku (Golden Pavilion), garden, and pond. Twentieth-century restoration of fourteenth-century building. Rokuon-ji (Kinkaku-ji), Kyoto.*

participants vied with one another to identify the places of origin of the different kinds of tea. Attendance at such gatherings was by no means restricted to priests and nobles. The mood of the time had changed, as can be judged from the description in the *Nijo-gawara Rakusho* (Scribblings at Nijo-gawara), publicly displayed notes in which the anonymous writer ironically criticized social trends in Kyoto: "The world is marked by confusion and lack of order. All authority is lost, and the possession or lack of inherited rank counts for nothing any more." The concept of undisciplined freedom hinted at here is none other than *basara*.

The term *basara*, which comes from *bazara* (Sanskrit, *vajra*), meaning "diamond," was applied to men who relished a life of luxury carried to excess. As a trend it was repeatedly condemned, but con-

demnation only served to increase its popularity. The central figure in the tea gatherings of the time was Kyogoku Doyo* (1306–72), who himself emerged as a protagonist of *basara* when he became powerful as "protector" of Omi Province (present Shiga Prefecture) during the days when the imperial lineage split in two opposed forces, the Northern and the Southern courts (1333–92). Illustrative of this trend is a description in the *Taiheiki*, a vivid war story completed in 1375 by an unknown author: "A group was formed in Kyoto that gathered every day to enjoy tea. Among its members were, first of all, the lay priest Sasaki Doyo [Kyogoku Doyo] and various daimyo living

---

* The names of all Japanese in the text are given, as in this case, in Japanese style (surname first).

2. Garden path (roji) of Tai-an tearoom, attributed to Sen no Rikyu. About 1582. Myoki-an temple, Kyoto Prefecture.

3. Shigure-tei (left) and Karakasa-tei (right) teahouses. About 1593–94. Kodai-ji, Kyoto.

in Kyoto. The climate at these gatherings was one of extravagant luxury, pleasure being indulged in for its own sake. To match the mood of the occasion, treasures both Chinese and Japanese were collected and laid out in display." The phrase "treasures both Chinese and Japanese were collected" expresses notably well that aspect of *basara* connected with tea.

Teahouses of the time are described in the *Kissa Orai* (Letters on Tea Drinking), one of the textbooks said to have been written by the Tendai priest Genne (also called Gen'e; 1269–1350) that contain, in letter form, descriptions of the manners and customs of the age when tea contests were in fashion. The book speaks of a pavilion surrounded by a garden. The upper floor constituted a gallery commanding a fine all-around view and served as

a place both for tea drinking and for viewing the moon. The description makes it sound like a teahouse of the Momoyama period (1568–1603). Though no example of this style remains today, we can get an idea of it from the Shigure-tei arbor at the Kodai-ji temple in Kyoto (Fig. 3), which serves as a rest house and as a site for viewing the scenery.

The extravagance of such a teahouse constituted the very essence of *basara,* and the display of utensils on the tea-utensil stand (*daisu*), a custom reputedly introduced by the Rinzai Zen priest Soseki (1276–1351; posthumously known as Muso Kokushi), was skillfully incorporated into the setting.

Doyo's successor as the leading exponent of *basara* was the third Ashikaga shogun, Yoshimitsu (1358–1408), whose construction of the Kinkaku,

4. "*Tea and Refreshments," from the narrative picture scroll* Boki Ekotoba *(Life of Priest Kaku-nyo). Colors on paper; height, 32.1 cm. 1351. Nishi Hongan-ji, Kyoto.*

or Golden Pavilion, at his Northern Hills Villa in Kyoto marked the culmination of the *basara* trend. By that time *basara* in the tea world was lapsing into a mere showy and copious display of wares from China and Korea. These wares, originally intended to be the formal furnishings of a room, had become the means for men of power to ex-

hibit their wealth. That *basara* had gone a long way toward becoming a mere formality is revealed in the practice of borrowing wares from other men of power for these displays, as the occasion demanded. Be all this as it may, the ardent pursuit of *basara* in the early stages of the tea parties may be said to have given rise to a new awareness of beauty.

CHAPTER TWO

Formal, Semiformal, Informal

THE ART IN THE tea ceremony was, in the final analysis, born of the tea meetings. It would seem, however, that in the early days of these tea meetings the sheer mass of goods flooding in from the Chinese mainland caused a loss of the true sense of beauty. The careful reconsidering of this situation received a fresh impetus soon after the Kakitsu Incident (1441), in which the sixth Ashikaga shogun, Yoshinori (1393–1441), was murdered by his vassal Akamatsu Mitsusuke (1381–1441)—a major turning point for the Ashikaga shogunate that marked a growing awareness among the common people, themselves influenced by the loss of authority. It was a time when the vast quantities of goods entering the country became disconnected from their practical use and ended up stored simply as assets in the repositories of the shogunate.

AMI, THE CONNOIS-SEURS OF THINGS CHINESE

Trade between Japan and Ming China (1368–1644) was increasing, and wares were brought into the country in profuse variety but with little discrimination. This was particularly true of Chinese paintings, interest in which stemmed not so much from artistic appreciation as from curiosity concerning the artists themselves. It followed that the greater part of the Chinese paintings were collected on the strength of the artists' renown back in China and their good connections with certain personalities in Japan.

This low level of appreciation is evidenced by the large portion of imported works that bore only an impressive signature and seal, the paintings themselves being of doubtful value. The painter Mu-ch'i (1176?–1239?) is a case in point. Of the works attributed to him, there remain today 104 scrolls (52 paintings of birds and animals, 32 paintings of Buddhist and Taoist priests, 2 landscapes, and 18 paintings on unknown themes), but those classifiable as unquestionably authentic by virtue of reliable provenance and on stylistic grounds amount to no more than three. These are the paintings that compose the triptych *Crane, Kannon, and Monkeys* (Fig. 5), preserved in the Daitoku-ji.

In reaction to this trend there came a moment when a pressing need was felt to distinguish between authentic values and spurious ones. This new consciousness was itself a point of departure for a deep search into the truth of beauty. In the Kitayama (Northern Hills) period—so called after the location of Ashikaga Yoshimitsu's villa—Yoshimitsu himself acted in the capacity of an appraiser with regard to Chinese paintings. The *Noritoki-kyo Ki*, the diary of the courtier Yamashina Noritoki, records the following event as having taken place at his residence in August 1406 of the lunar calendar: "I sent a messenger to Kin'ami with a request that he investigate the authenticity of a painting of nymphs brought over from China. He judged the work to have been painted recently in Japan." We can see that already by that time Kin'ami was

5. Kannon *(Avalokitesvara), by Mu-ch'i (Fa-ch'ang), from the hanging-scroll triptych* Crane, Kannon, and Monkeys. *Ink on paper; height, 172 cm.; width, 98 cm. Southern Sung dynasty, twelfth or thirteenth century. Daitoku-ji, Kyoto.*

6. Tokonoma of Tai-an tearoom, attributed ▷ *to Sen no Rikyu. About 1582. Myoki-an temple, Kyoto Prefecture. (See also Figure 196.)*

known as a specialist in the appraisal of paintings.

Subsequently, with the advent of the Higashi-yama period—named after the Eastern Hills, where the eighth Ashikaga shogun, Yoshimasa (1435–90), built the Silver Pavilion at his villa—a reappraisal of the quality of Chinese paintings could no longer be delayed, and the need arose for a new assessment of the collections stored in the shogunal repositories. In response to this need, expert connoisseurs fast rose to positions of eminence. The men most suited to the task were thought to be the *doboshu*, a group of attendants then attached to the Eastern Hills Villa and engaged daily in the purchase and protection of art objects from China. These men commonly added to their names the suffix *ami*, short for Amida Butsu, an honorary Buddhist title conferred on monks and artists. Hence they were known as the Amis. In the *Jojo Kikigaki Sho*, records of the old customs and manners of the samurai,

written in 1528 by Ise no Sadayori, we find a passage to the effect that Sen'ami and Soami (1472–1525) were commissioners for Chinese goods, whose task it was to "judge the good and the bad" and to label the goods as being of "high, middle, or low quality." Besides this, it was their duty to "act as envoys for the court nobles, daimyo, and other men of power," conveying gifts in observance of the custom of celebrating the first fruits of the harvest on the first day of August of the lunar calendar. This indicates that it was in the days of Ashikaga Yoshimasa's rule that the position of the commissioners for Chinese goods took on a special importance.

The *Chaki Meibutsu Shu* (Collection of Renowned Tea Utensils) of 1421 records the name of Maiami, father of the celebrated artist Noami (1397–1471). In succession after him three other Amis—namely, Noami, Geiami (1431–85), and Soami (1472–1525)

7. *Tea bowl called Tsutsuizutsu. O-ido ware; diameter, 14.5 cm. Yi dynasty,
fifteenth or sixteenth century. Saga family, Ishikawa Prefecture.*

8. Tea bowl called Muichibutsu, by Tanaka Chojiro. Red Raku ware; diameter, 11 cm. Late sixteenth century. Egawa family, Hyogo Prefecture.

9. *Flower container. Iga ware;
height, 28 cm. Sixteenth or
seventeenth century. Fujiwara
family, Tokyo.*

10. *Garden of En-an teahouse,* ▷
*designed by Furuta Oribe. About
1640–55. Yabunouchi school of
tea, Kyoto.*

11. *Interior view of Mittan tearoom, showing server's seat at left and tokonoma at right. Designed by Kobori Enshu. About 1628–39. Ryoko-in, Daitoku-ji, Kyoto.*

12. *Tea bowl called Fujisan (Mount Fuji), by Hon'ami Koetsu. White Raku ware; diameter, 11.6 cm. First half of seventeenth century. Sakai family, Tokyo. (See also Figure 69.)*

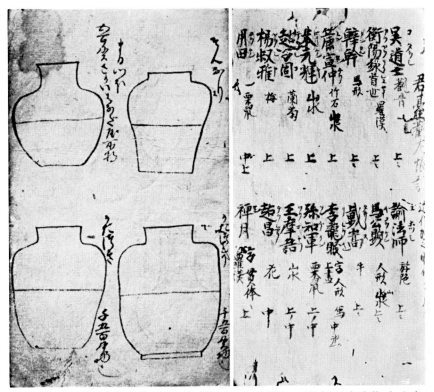

13. *Pages from* Kundaikan Sa-u Choki *(Catalogue of Ashikaga Yoshimasa's Collection), by Noami. 1566. Kofuku-ji, Nara.*

—began their activities. In August 1443, by order of the honorary retired emperor Gosuko (1372–1456), Noami passed judgment on the paintings of hawks kept in the Jushin-in temple, his conclusion being that they were "clearly of Chinese origin, artist unknown." From this we may infer that by this time the family had already become the highest authority in the connoisseurship of art objects.

In this way, under Ashikaga Yoshimasa, the three Amis—the relatively short-lived Geiami, preceded by Noami and followed by Soami—were all in turn engaged in the administration and appraisal of the shogunal collections. It was in connection with this assignment of theirs that the *Kundaikan Sa-u Choki* (Fig. 13), the first version of which was prepared by Noami and the next by Soami in 1511, became an extremely important standard for connoisseurs. This book comprised a list of im-

portant Chinese painters, descriptions of various styles of tokonoma (alcove) decorations that appeared in the shoguns' mansions, and suggestions concerning the appreciation and arrangement of Chinese wares. The influence of the Amis spread rapidly, and it was not long before the combination and arrangement of tea utensils for display on the utensil stand came within the scope of their work. A proper arrangement of wares was indispensable for creating a suitable atmosphere at any place of entertainment, and the prowess of the three Amis became the focus of attention. They were now esteemed as the absolute authority, even from the standpoint of entertainments like tea gatherings and flower arrangement. In a word, what constituted the beauty of tea was precisely the way of making these arrangements. For the Amis, this meant stressing the correct rule of giving highest

regard to Chinese goods. Theirs was indeed the beauty of the "formal," which transmitted the standard for the formal layout of the drawing room.

JUKO, THE FATHER OF THE TEA CEREMONY

It was not long before the man later to be venerated as the founder of the *cha-no-yu* (tea ceremony), Murata Juko (1422–1502), made his appearance in the Eastern Hills Villa, where Ashikaga Yoshimasa lived surrounded by his band of Amis. We read in the *Yamashina Kotokuni-kyo Ke Zakki* (Miscellaneous Records of the Courtier Yamashina Kotokuni's Family) that during the fifth lunar month of 1468, while he was living in Nara, Juko placed an order with the Yamashina family of Kyoto for the making of an *oguchi-bakama,* a pair of skirtlike trousers for ceremonial wear. At the time, Juko was forty-six years of age. In all likelihood he felt the necessity of being provided with suitable dress in keeping with ancient court practice, since many of the Kyoto nobles were now moving to Nara to escape the Onin War (1467–77), a decade of conflict among powerful daimyo over the selection of the successor to Yoshimasa. It is believed that Juko, born in Nara as the son of a blind priest and from his early years a monk of the Shomyo-ji temple, had grown up with a powerful merchant family in Nara, whence he probably received the name Murata, and this may have been another reason why he needed formal attire. During or after the conflict he was apparently given an opportunity to go up to Kyoto. By that time he had already been granted a copy of the *Kundaikan Sa-u Choki* by Noami, then well advanced in years. Noami had gone down to Nara, it is thought, to escape the civil war and remained there until the time of his death at the Hase-dera temple in 1471. For Juko, the acquisition of such a teacher was an experience of deep significance and in all likelihood provided the deciding motive for his move to Kyoto. He

14. *"Rinkan Cha-no-yu," from the narrative picture scroll* Sairei Zoshi *(Stories of Festive Rites). Colors on paper; dimensions of entire scroll: height, 19.6 cm.; length, 614.9 cm. Fifteenth century. Maeda Ikutoku-kai, Tokyo.*

15. Yuteki *(oil spot)* tem-moku *tea bowl. Diameter, 12.2 cm. Southern Sung dynasty, thirteenth century.*

went primarily to practice Zen meditation with Ikkyu Sojun (1394–1481), abbot of the Daitoku-ji temple since 1474, severe critic of decadent Zen practices, and promoter of popular forms of Zen. At the same time, Juko sought to serve Ashikaga Yoshimasa at the Eastern Hills Villa. It is likely that he gained access to the shogun's court through the good offices of Soami, whose father, Noami, had been Juko's master.

Nara, where Juko had been brought up, was at the time the scene of lewd tea parties known as *rinkan cha-no-yu,* which combined tea drinking with bathing (Fig. 14). In a word, the *basara* tea world was still alive, and Juko probably had contact with it. One promoter of this kind of tea party was Furuichi Tanehide, a monk-soldier who held high rank among the heads of his village and was attached to the Kofuku-ji temple in Nara. One of his pastimes was to organize magnificent and novel parties such as those staged in the bath. His younger brother, Furuichi Sumitane (1459–1508), titular

governor of Harima Province (present Hyogo Prefecture), owned some thirty varieties of rare utensils and was not only regarded a master of *suki* (artistic taste) but was also termed Juko's most outstanding disciple. Juko, too, seems to have been familiar with the *rinkan cha-no-yu* and hence with the popular tea atmosphere in Nara.

Juko's tea thus consisted of a blend of the two types of tea he himself had experienced, one centered on Chinese wares, his inheritance from Noami, and the other based on the tea gatherings. The statement "I have no taste for the full moon," which the Noh playwright and actor Komparu Zempo (1454–c. 1520) attributed to Juko, suggests that Juko felt more moved by a moon half hidden in the clouds than by one viewed in all its roundness. This statement is thought to contain a veiled criticism of the model of ideal tea centered on Chinese objects. The same idea is found in the following words, which Zempo also attributes to Juko: "I think that Japanese utensils like those from Ise

16. Taihi *(tortoise shell)* temmoku *tea bowl. Diameter, 11.6 cm. Southern Sung dynasty, twelfth or thirteenth century. Miyawaki family, Tokyo.*

17. *Tea bowl called Shibata. Blue Ido ware; diameter, 15.2 cm. Formerly owned by Shibata Katsuie. Yi dynasty, sixteenth century. Nezu Art Museum, Tokyo.*

Province [present Mie Prefecture] and Bizen Province [present Okayama Prefecture], if they are attractive and skillfully made, are superior to Chinese ones." These observations point to a rediscovery of things Japanese, long overshadowed by Chinese goods—that is to say, a rediscovery of the beauty in what is not completely perfect as opposed to what is ideal. Yet even this stipulated that the wares be "attractive and skillfully made." What was sought was a creation shaped by originality and inventiveness. In his "Letter of the Mind" (Fig. 18), written to Furuichi Sumitane, Juko states that "one point of exceeding importance in the pursuit of the way of tea is the need to efface the boundary line separating Chinese wares, simply because they are Chinese, from those made in Japan. In other words, the wares of both countries should be integrated." The cultural ideal of a Sino-Japanese synthesis, later to bloom in the Momoyama period, was here beginning to show its head.

The heir to Juko's philosophy of tea was Soju, who lived among the townspeople in a bustling row of houses in Shimogyo, a district in the southern part of Kyoto. In the autumn of 1526, the *renga* (linked verse) poet Socho (1448–1532) visited Soju's hermitage, which comprised a 4.5-mat and a 6-mat room and was at the time often referred to as the Shimogyo Cha-no-yu. Struck by the elegant scene of five or six ivy leaves fallen within the low hedge, he was inspired to compose the following *hokku*, or the first stanza of a *renga* series:

> After last night's storm—
> Picking up the first maple leaves.

Despite a storm the previous night, Socho found only five or six leaves on the ground, which suggests that Soju had purposely left them there when sweeping up. This attitude of mind gives us a deep insight into Juko's statement "I have no taste for the full moon" and was to be summed up much later, in modern times, by Okakura Tenshin (1862–

1913; see Chapter Seven), for whom tea was "the worship of the imperfect." A similar story concerning the famous tea master Rikyu and his teacher, Jo-o, serves to further illustrate this central thought. On a certain occasion Jo-o sought Rikyu's opinion about a garden that had been swept immaculately clean. To his companion's great astonishment, Rikyu reacted by shaking some leaves off a tree. He was eighteen or nineteen years of age at the time.

To return to Soju's hermitage, even a court noble of the time could exclaim: "I am deeply impressed by this scene. Here, in the very heart of the city, I have the impression of being in the country. Soju deserves to be called a hermit and is undoubtedly a driving force behind the *suki* of today." And it was not only Soju. Like him, his disciples from Shimogyo, Sochin and Sogo, built hermitages in Gojo Matsubara in Kyoto. This new life of the "man of artistic taste" (*sukisha*) also won the hearts of the merchants of Sakai, the commercial city near Osaka.

JO-O AND RIKYU   Takeno Jo-o (1502–55) was born the heir of a wealthy tanner of Sakai. In 1525 he moved to Kyoto in order to get himself an education. He was then twenty-three years of age. He studied Japanese poetry with Sanjonishi Sanetaka (1455–1537), a man whom even the aristocracy of his day esteemed for his great erudition, and in Shimogyo took lessons in Juko's style of tea with Sochin and Sogo. It is interesting to follow his reactions. As a merchant from Sakai, Jo-o was better prepared than Juko to reach close to the lives of the common people, for Juko was permanently influenced by his life at the Eastern Hills Villa. In the *Nambo Roku* (Records of Nambo), a veritable bible of the *cha-no-yu* written by Nambo Sokei, a rich merchant of Sakai and disciple of Sen no Rikyu, the following explanation is given: "For tea drinking, Juko made use for the first time of a 4.5-mat room. He used glossy light-yellow paper to cover the walls, installed a joistless ceiling made of pine boards, and constructed a pyramidal roof covered with small wooden shingles. On the wall of the six-foot tokonoma he hung a rare and treasured calligraphy scroll by the Chi-

nese Zen priest Yuan-wu [c. 1063–1135] and on its floor displayed a tea-utensil stand [*daisu*]. Then he provided a sunken hearth, the rims of which were decorated with a fine wooden frame [*kyudai*]. Generally he placed in his room the same ornaments as in a *shoin* [formal reception room] of samurai taste, though reducing them in number." Not even a man of the stature of Juko could destroy the tradition of the decorative *daisu* adopted by Noami for use in the palatial room of the samurai aristocracy. On the other hand, the same *Nambo Roku* states that "Jo-o changed to using a 4.5-mat room with plain clay walls in place of the light-yellow paper used in Juko's time and a bamboo-lattice ceiling in place of the wooden one. He also did away with the wainscot on the paper sliding doors. To the base of the tokonoma frame he either gave a thin coat of lacquer or left it bare in order to allow a direct view of the plain wood. This room he designated *so*, or 'informal,' and he did not ornament it with a *daisu*."

Jo-o undoubtedly brought tea a big step closer to the simple world of ordinary people. His style revealed an "informal" beauty, seen as a leap from the "formal" (*shin*) that bypassed the "semiformal" (*gyo*) style. If formal beauty is considered as the standardized decorating of a room, then Juko and Sochin, who half destroyed this tradition, deserve to be called semiformal, and Jo-o becomes informal. Rikyu once said that "the basis of the *cha-no-yu* is the *daisu*, but if we look for the heart of the *cha-no-yu* we will find it nowhere other than in the small 'informal' room." He may be said to have added much greater depth to Jo-o's informal style of beauty.

Sen no Rikyu (1521–91), whose real name was Sen Soeki, was the grandson of Sen'ami, entertainment attendant (*doboshu*) at the court of Ashikaga Yoshimasa and colleague of Noami and Soami. He was the first son of Sen Yohei, an affluent "warehouse owner" (*nayashu*), or merchant, who dealt with the fishing industry in Sakai. He took his lessons in the tea ceremony under Kitamuki Dochin (1502–?), who worked in the same leather business as Jo-o and inherited his tea style from Soami. In 1540 Rikyu was introduced to Jo-o, who had just

18. *"Letter of the Mind," by Murata Juko. Ink on paper. Fifteenth century. Hirase family, Kyoto.*

19. *View of Ashikaga Yoshimasa's Dojinsai* shoin *room, showing staggered shelves* ▷
at left and tsuke shoin *at right. 1486. Togu-do, Jisho-ji (Ginkaku-ji), Kyoto.*

returned to Sakai, and immediately became his disciple. His tea style not only derived from those of Juko and Jo-o but also included the mastery of the *cha-no-yu* at the Eastern Hills Villa. His life is all too well known. After completing his period of apprenticeship in Sakai in the company of his tea friends Imai Sokyu (1520–93) and Tsuda Sokyu (?–1591)—together with whom he was later known as one of the Three Grand Masters of the Way of Tea—he was soon leading a relatively dedicated life as grand tea master (*chasho*) in the service of the famous warrior-daimyo Oda Nobunaga (1534–82), with whom he remained from 1570 to 1573. Following this, as head tea master (*chado*) under Toyotomi Hideyoshi (1536–98), the military dictator who finally unified Japan after the long "age of warring provinces," which had lasted since the Onin War, Rikyu came to exert an influence that was vast despite its unobtrusiveness. It was during this stage, one of profound significance in his life, that he began his opposition to the fancy for gold and gaudiness in the *cha-no-yu* of his day, an extravagance whereby those in authority sought to make a display of their power. And he did it by laying heavy emphasis on the *soan cha-no-yu*, or tea ceremony in a thatched hermitage, designed to create a natural atmosphere for tea in contrast with the atmosphere of the town. As a result, he was later ordered by the angry Hideyoshi to terminate his life by seppuku. In the interval, in the autumn of 1587, the Great Kitano Tea Party, conceived by Hideyoshi and staged by Rikyu, provided the setting for the supreme drama. Its closing after only one day because an uprising occurred in Higo Province in Kyushu—and because Rikyu was robbing Hideyoshi of the limelight—constituted perhaps a symbolic prelude to Rikyu's tragic ending. The ideal to which he devoted the major part of

his life was to further and protect to the utmost within his power the *soan cha-no-yu.*

THE DAISU TEA advocated by Rikyu as "the basis of the *cha-no-yu*" originated in the tea-utensil cabinet (*cha-no-yu-dana*) used in the Ashikaga court. It was in this cabinet that various tea utensils were properly arranged and kept. For example, at the Muromachi Palace of the shogun Yoshinori there was one in the pantry connected with the living quarters; at the Ogawa Villa of Yoshimasa, in the "east lower room" adjoining the audience chamber; and at his Eastern Hills Villa, in the "west tea-boiling area" in the Ishiyama Room of the audience suite. The *cha-no-yu* cabinet was placed in the *cha-no-yu ma*, or "tea-boiling room," and it was customary for the *doboshu* to keep the utensils in it clean and to make preparations for the ceremony. The *cha-no-yu* room was not itself a place for

the reception of guests but simply an anteroom for readying the ceremony. Located in a secondary position vis-à-vis the main drawing room, at times it was even one step below floor level, and its use was reserved for people of lower class. The tea prepared there was carried to the guest room, which was adorned with a board-floored tokonoma, a *tsuke shoin* (a window whose broad sill served as a writing desk), and ornamental staggered shelves (*chigaidana*). This total separation of the room where tea was prepared from the room where it was served is an outstanding characteristic of "palace tea."

FROM PALACE TEA TO TEA IN THE SITTING ROOM

The standard width of the *cha-no-yu* cabinet was 1 *ken* (6 *shaku*, or about 1.82 meters)—the length of one tatami mat—and it was fitted with either removable or fixed shelves. With the aid of this cabinet,

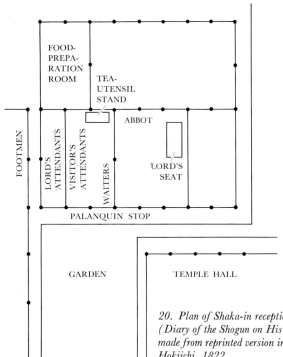

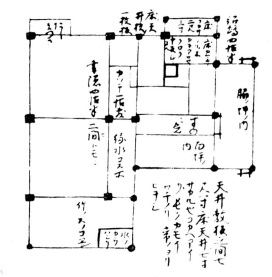

21. Plan of Takeno Jo-o's 4.5-mat tearoom, from Yamanoue Soji Densho *(Writings of Yamanoue Soji). 1588.*

20. Plan of Shaka-in reception room, from Muromachi-dono Kami Daigo Gotozan Nikki *(Diary of the Shogun on His Visit to Kami Daigo Temple). Original dated 1518; present copy made from reprinted version in* Gunsho Ruiju *(An Assortment of Writings), edited by Hanawa Hokiichi, 1822.*

which was lavishly decorated in Chinese style and which in itself sufficed to constitute the formal lay-out of a room, the *cha-no-yu* could be performed simply by arranging all the utensils in it. With the disappearance of the *cha-no-yu* cabinet, however, important functions it had performed became more firmly established than before, one served by the tokonoma and another by the sunken hearth. A new setting for the *cha-no-yu* was thus born, which hastened the emergence of the "sitting-room *cha-no-yu*." The decline of the *cha-no-yu* cabinet and the emergence of the *daisu* (tea-utensil stand) heralded the change from the "palace tea" favored by cour-tiers and the samurai aristocracy to "sitting-room tea." The latter would witness host and guests seated in one room that combined the functions of the preparation room and the guests' drawing room.

The earliest literature concerning sitting-room tea is found in Soami's *Cha Densho* (Writings on Tea), dated 1523 in the colophon and presently preserved in the Tokyo National Museum (Fig. 23). Referring mainly to the method using a utensil tray and a brazier mat as well as the *daisu,* it also alludes to the handling of old-style shelves that con-jure up memories of the *cha-no-yu* cabinet. Though not without some doubt, this book is considered to include also the tea customs of Juko's age. All the tearooms illustrated in it are of the 4.5-mat type, some of them fitted for the "right-hand style" and others for the "left-hand style." That is to say, the position of the hearth and the tokonoma deter-mined the seating of the guests, the tokonoma placed either to their right or to their left. It seems, however, that the tokonoma measured not 1 *ken* (1.82 meters) but 5 *shaku* (1.52 meters), a highly

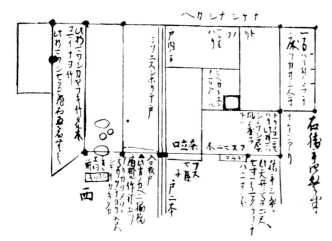

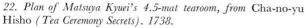

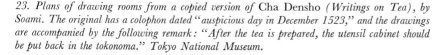

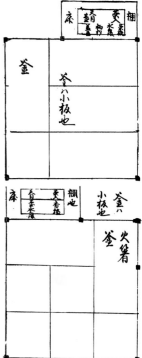

22. *Plan of Matsuya Kyuei's 4.5-mat tearoom, from* Cha-no-yu Hisho *(Tea Ceremony Secrets). 1738.*

23. *Plans of drawing rooms from a copied version of* Cha Densho *(Writings on Tea), by Soami. The original has a colophon dated "auspicious day in December 1523," and the drawings are accompanied by the following remark: "After the tea is prepared, the utensil cabinet should be put back in the tokonoma." Tokyo National Museum.*

unnatural feature that does not match the use in Soami's day. As for the merchants and other towns-people, this sitting-room style of tea provided a starting point from which to develop the trend of informalization.

For the townsmen, the opportunity to exchange greetings with the nobility was one of the enjoyable highlights of the tea meetings. The knowledge of manners required of them on such occasions formed the basis for the etiquette of the tea ceremony. They saw in the *daisu* and the *meibutsu* (renowned objects) two symbols of the aristocracy. An idea in vogue in Jo-o's time held that only a man in possession of *meibutsu* could build a 4.5-mat room with a toko-noma. And it was in the midst of this trend that Jo-o's 4.5-mat room made its appearance. This is recorded by Yamanoue Soji (1544–90), Rikyu's best disciple and a rich merchant of Sakai (Fig.

21). The room faced north, with a veranda at-tached to the entrance. The posts were of Japanese cypress, and above white-papered walls stretched a simple rustic ceiling of thin boards. The room was furnished with a 6-*shaku* tokonoma. Jo-o may have found inspiration for this kind of orderly de-sign in the mansion of the poet and calligrapher Sanjonishi Sanetaka and also in the drawing rooms for poetry contests, where he was a frequent visitor after his move to Kyoto. At any rate, this style of room was deemed most appropriate for holding tea parties for the purpose of meeting the nobility and handling *meibutsu*. The structure of the room de-serves attention in that the height of the lintel was "less than usual." The slight lowering of the lintel over the entrance was the most basic structural rule concerning the tearoom and would later be emphasized even more in the *nijiri-guchi* (literally,

24. *Interior view of Zangetsu-tei teahouse, designed by Sen Shoan. Originally built in late sixteenth century; rebuilt in 1909. Omote Senke school of tea, Kyoto.*

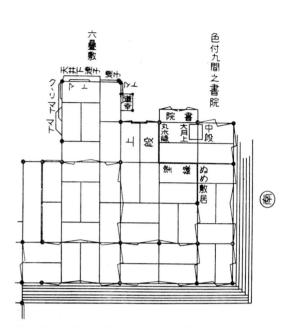

25. *Plan of Colored Shoin in Sen no Rikyu's Juraku residence, from* Rikyu Koji Juraku no Taku Zutori *(Diagram of Layman Rikyu's Juraku Residence). Omote Senke school of tea, Kyoto.*

"wriggling-through entrance"), the low sliding-door aperture by which guests enter the tearoom. This important feature had its starting point in Jo-o's 4.5-mat room.

Matsuya Kyuei, a merchant of Nara, also built a tearoom modeled on Jo-o's 4.5-mat style. The height of the lower edge of the lintel measured 5.715 *shaku* (slightly over 1.73 meters) from the threshold, and only that portion of the lintel facing the interior of the room was furnished with a filletlike ornamental band. The square posts measured 0.28 *shaku* (about 8.5 centimeters) with 0.01 *shaku* (about 3 millimeters) shaved off the corners, and their special feature was "the irregular grain facing inward." Similar posts appear in Jo-o's 4.5-mat room, or "the sitting room bequeathed by Jo-o to Soeki [Rikyu]," as described in the *Cha-no-yu Hisho* (Tea Ceremony Secrets), which contains

three hundred rules and explanatory notes of the Sekishu school of tea. In Matsuya's room, the northerly orientation, the "left-hand style," and the 6-*shaku* tokonoma were the same as in Jo-o's room, but the walls were of clay. By Jo-o's standards this tearoom would probably be classified as informal. Though unfinished logs were not yet used in the tearooms of Jo-o's time, the use of pillars with "the irregular grain facing inward" set a precedent, and the time would soon be ripe for the change to barely finished logs.

Records of tea parties in the Muromachi period (1336–1568) make frequent mention of the direction in which the room faces. The reason for this is that tearooms of those times had no windows at all, and the only source of light was the guests' entrance. The degree of light or darkness inside the room was thus determined by the way the room

26. *Lean-to over earth-floored area of Tai-an tearoom, attributed to Sen no Rikyu. About 1582. Myoki-an temple, Kyoto Prefecture.*

27. *Interior view of Tai-an tearoom, attributed to Sen no Rikyu. About 1582. Myoki-an temple, Kyoto Prefecture.*

faced. Ikenaga Sosaku, a disciple of Jo-o's, explains in his writings that in an overly bright room the utensils look too coarse, while the guest himself is less prepared psychologically to appreciate things than he is in the state of interior calm induced by subdued light. Thus, in order to achieve the right degree of illumination "for the utensils to be viewed in all their worth," the tearoom should face north. In this, Ikenaga probably inherited the opinion of Jo-o, who preferred a room facing north.

Through the careful planning of measurements and materials and the search for delicate lighting effects, the spatial structure of the tearoom was determined along general lines in Jo-o's 4.5-mat room. According to Yamanoue Soji, Jo-o's style of room was imitated by "people of Kyoto and Sakai who own Chinese wares," including men like Imai Sokyu, Soeki (Rikyu), Takeno Soga (1550–1614),

who was the eldest son of Jo-o, Tsuda Sokyu, and Soji himself.

Rikyu's tearoom, too, had its origin in the imitation of Jo-o's 4.5-mat room. The tearoom in his Sakai mansion followed that pattern, as apparently did the one he built in the Shisei-bo (see Foldout 1), the priest's residence at the Todai-ji temple, which has been preserved in the form of stand-up paper models. One of the salient features of all tearooms at the time was the presence of a veranda in front of the entrance. Early tea writings take the veranda for granted in explaining the etiquette of entry into the teahouse and show that the guests left their swords there before entry and took a short rest there during the intermission when the host prepared for the next part of the tea ceremony. Thus it served the purpose of the later sword rack and bench and was intimately related to the func-

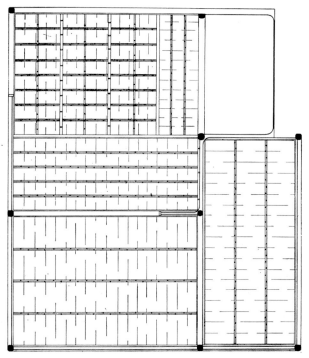

28. Detail of ceiling of Tai-an tearoom, attributed to Sen no Rikyu, with calligraphy on tablet by Hoshuku (d. 1727), twelfth abbot of the Kotsu-ji. About 1582. Myoki-an temple, Kyoto Prefecture.

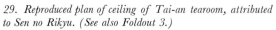

29. Reproduced plan of ceiling of Tai-an tearoom, attributed to Sen no Rikyu. (See also Foldout 3.)

tion of the tearoom and the etiquette that prevailed there. It is recorded in the Momoyama-period tea book *Sencha Shu* (Hermit's Tea) that in 1583, at his residence in Sakai, Rikyu himself was still using a tearoom with this kind of veranda attached.

In Jo-o's tearoom, the veranda faced the front courtyard garden, while the side courtyard garden was formed by the path. According to *Senrin*, a book published in 1612 advocating a return to the spirit of Rikyu and Juko—a current in vogue at the time —no trees or stones were placed in the front courtyard garden in order not to distract the guests' attention and likewise to enable them "to devote themselves wholeheartedly to the *cha-no-yu* and to the appreciation of the fine *meibutsu* utensils." It was considered better to plant grass and a few trees in the garden facing the adjoining room or in the area of the basin where the guests washed their hands. Thus it was along the path, rather, that a gardenlike scene gradually took shape. In the long run, though, the path did not lose its function as an access to the tearoom.

Within a short time the garden path had advanced right up to the front of the tearoom. The veranda disappeared and was replaced by the eaves overhanging the unfloored area in front of the house. With the elimination of the veranda a bench made its appearance on the garden path, a sword rack was devised, and the entrance gave way to a *nijiri-guchi*. In a word, the exterior appearance of the teahouse underwent a great transformation. From the standpoint of architectural form, the removal of the veranda signified a complete break with the *shoin* (reception room) of palatial architecture, and the way thus lay open for a free pursuit of the informal. Rikyu has left us the plan of a 4.5-mat room with an earth-floored area (Fig. 188) in place of the old veranda, and in various aspects this plan reflects the transitional nature of the period. The earth-floored area disappeared in turn, with the outer wall taken off, evolving into a kind of midway space between the interior and the exterior of the room. The steppingstones of the garden path led through this space and right up to the *nijiri-guchi,* which thus became a direct meeting point of mat and garden. What emerged was a place for the *cha-no-yu* that unified the garden and the tearoom, and the external appearance of the *soan* (thatched hermitage) achieved its form.

THE SPIRIT OF WABI   It is related in the previously noted *Nambo Roku* that in Jo-o's presence Rikyu for the first time performed the *cha-no-yu* in which the utensils were brought into the room and placed directly on the mat. It is uncertain when this took place, yet the introduction of such a style, with the performance following the bringing in of the utensils, and the consequent discontinuation of the use of shelves for the utensils, including the *daisu*, undoubtedly had a considerable influence on the informalization of the tearoom. Even in Rikyu's tearooms, however, this process of informalization was not achieved at one stroke. The 4.5-mat tearoom with an earth-floored area mentioned above had such features of informalization as an arched entrance (*kato-guchi*) for the host and openings left in the clay-plastered walls to expose the understructure in the form of latticework windows (*shitaji mado*), but the square posts with shaved-off corners and the 6-*shaku* tokonoma were retained. The 4.5-mat room he built on the grounds of the Daitoku-ji temple, probably about the year 1582, featured a 5-*shaku* tokonoma whose walls were covered with light-gray paper— an indication that not even Rikyu was able easily to overstep the tradition of the 6-*shaku* tokonoma with papered walls. From the time he was named grand tea master under Toyotomi Hideyoshi, however, the transformation of the tearoom into the shape of the small, unassuming *soan* proceeded very rapidly. The *soan*-style hut with a smaller room (*koma*), usually of three mats, soon came into great vogue, reaching the peak of its popularity in the years 1586–87.

As a consequence, the idea that linked the size of the room and the presence or absence of a tokonoma with the possession of *meibutsu* was overthrown. A case in point is that of the base of the tokonoma frame. It had been said that "those who own *gomotsu* [shogun's property] treasures or *meibutsu* should lacquer the base without fail, while those who own none may leave it plain." To this,

Rikyu countered that "nowadays this is a matter of personal taste." He also stressed that "a scroll hung in the tokonoma on a rough wall looks very interesting," and he transformed the tokonoma by covering the walls with clay. The 4.5-mat rooms he built for the Great Kitano Tea Party and in his residence on the grounds of Hideyoshi's castle-palace Juraku-dai (see Foldout 1) show that informalization had attained completion.

Yet Rikyu's informalization of the tearoom did not represent merely a revolution in design. It further included a qualitative change that touched on the very essence of the *cha-no-yu*. While making the *daisu cha-no-yu* his teaching principle, Rikyu succeeded in freeing his "small informal room" (tearoom smaller than the 4.5-mat room) from its control. This he did by informalizing the room and reducing its size. The spirit of the *soan* was carried to its extreme—that is, *wabi*, which may be rendered as "finding satisfaction in poverty"—until it stood on even terms with the *daisu cha-no-yu* and finally even surpassed it.

The Tai-an tearoom in the Myoki-an temple (Fig. 6), located not far from Kyoto, has many of the same structural features that characterized the 2-mat room in Rikyu's residence at Juraku-dai. Besides, it is the only remaining building that can definitely be attributed to Rikyu. In this small 2-mat room with its rough walls, a fine compositional technique is freely and accurately used to convey an extremely taut feeling of space. The structure of the *murodoko* (a deep tokonoma with clay-plastered walls), with the three large knots staring out, as it were, from the log lining the base of the frame, indicates a culmination of *wabi* modeling achieved through passionate energy in the search for the ultimate. Toyotomi Hideyoshi wasted no time in having such a 2-mat room built in the Yamazato-maru compound in Osaka Castle, and even the golden tearoom, where the display of his gorgeous utensils served to show off his supreme authority, belonged in the scale of the 3-mat "small informal room." So powerful was the idea that gave shape to *wabi* that even the man who had it in his hands to steer his country's fortunes was unconsciously forced to restrain his taste.

UTENSILS OF FORMAL TEA

The reception-room (*shoin*) *cha-no-yu* performed for the shogun Ashikaga Yoshimasa at the Eastern Hills Villa by the *doboshu* Noami and Soami is known as formal (*shin*) tea. The utensils and decorations used for the staging of this solemn ceremony, complete with a rigid observance of all the formalities of etiquette, were purely of Chinese origin. Such were the paintings of the Sung (960–1279) and Yuan (1280–1368) dynasties and the *temmoku* tea bowls of the Sung, a variety that the priests of Buddhist temples on Mount T'ienmu in northwestern Chekiang Province first used as vessels for eating. This formal tea, in other words, was the "*cha-no-yu* of the Chinese wares," and Chinese art played the leading role in the refined salon where Yoshimasa held sway.

The Japanese admiration for Chinese art dated from early times, and already in the days of Yoshi-

31. Evening Glow over a Fishing Village, *attributed to Mu-ch'i (Fa-ch'ang).*
One of a set of eight hand scrolls entitled Eight Views of the Hsiao and the Hsiang.
Ink on paper; height, 33 cm.; length, 113 cm. Southern Sung dynasty, twelfth or
thirteenth century. Nezu Art Museum, Tokyo.

◁ 30. *Interior view of Jo-an tearoom, showing central post and hearth. Designed by*
Oda Uraku. About 1618. Shiroyama Villa, Mitsui family, Kanagawa Prefecture.

masa many outstanding Chinese paintings filled the shogunal repositories, as indicated in the *Gomotsu Goe Mokuroku* (Inventory of Wares and Paintings in the Possession of the Shoguns). It was in this Higashiyama period that lovers of art became aware of the orthodox beauty in the goods from China and proceeded to use them as utensils to achieve an orderly system of the *cha-no-yu.*

The extent to which the artistic taste (*suki*) for Chinese goods prevailed at the time is made clear in the *Kundaikan Sa-u Choki.* One's first feeling on reading this ancient catalogue is that, in the interval extending from the Kitayama period to the Higashiyama period, it was the appreciation and above all the connoisseurship of Chinese objects that constituted the main object of this *suki.* All the wares imported from China: paintings, ceramics, lacquerware, dyed and woven goods, and metalwork—in a word, all the items required to enhance

the solemnity of the *shoin*—were duly set in order. The way in which the paintings were handled differed markedly from the way in which handicraft goods were treated. Objects other than paintings—even such gemlike utensils as the *yohen temmoku* tea bowls (Fig. 34), famous for their iridescent glaze and esteemed priceless even at that time—were ultimately treated simply as vessels. The paintings, on the other hand, were regarded with great respect and accorded the best treatment, perhaps because they were to be displayed in the board-floored niche, the precursor of the tokonoma. Likewise, in the case of art objects other than paintings, there was practically no need for connoisseurs to determine their authenticity or that of the makers, whereas in the case of paintings this was essential. Since both Noami and Soami were authorities on the subject, they devoted many pages in the first chapter of their *Kundaikan Sa-u Choki* to drawing

32. Dove and Peach Blossoms, *by Emperor Hui Tsung. Colors on silk; height, 29 cm.; width, 26 cm. Northern Sung dynasty, 1107.*

33. Monkey, *attributed to Mao Sung. Colors on silk; height, 45.8 cm.; width, 36.6 cm. Southern Sung dynasty, twelfth or thirteenth century. Manju-in, Kyoto.* ▷

up a record of Chinese paintings according to their different levels of quality—an occupation in which they probably took great pride. At all events, large sections of the *Gomotsu Goe Mokuroku* and the *Kundaikan Sa-u Choki* were taken up with the description of Chinese paintings, leaving no doubt that these were the object of intense admiration.

The *Gomotsu Goe Mokuroku* is, as stated earlier, a catalogue of the collection stored in the shogunal repositories comprising mainly the Chinese paintings owned by Ashikaga Yoshimitsu. Compiled by Noami and recorded by Soami, it lists many famous paintings preserved until the present time. Included among them are the hanging-scroll triptych *Crane, Kannon, and Monkeys* (Fig. 5) by Mu-ch'i (Fa-ch'ang), the Chinese painter who so greatly influenced Japanese ink painting. Also included are four scrolls from his *Eight Views of the Hsiao and the Hsiang: Returning Sails on a Vast Bay* (Fig. 169),

Temple Bell in the Evening Mist (Fig. 42), *Evening Glow over a Fishing Village* (Fig. 31), and *Wild Geese Descending over a Sandy Plain.* From the *Eight Views of the Hsiao and the Hsiang* by Yu-chien, a contemporary of Mu-ch'i's whose style also had a major influence on Japanese ink painters, three scrolls are listed: *Mountain Village in a Fine Haze* (Fig. 138), *Returning Sails on a Vast Bay,* and *Autumn Moon over Lake Tungt'ing.* Yet another painting is the *Duck* by Emperor Hui Tsung (1082–1135), a Northern Sung painter known for his landscapes and flower-and-bird paintings and considered the best of the emperor-painters. It is presently in the collection of the Goto Art Museum in Tokyo. The *Tsuda Sokyu Cha-no-yu Nikki* (Tea Diary of Tsuda Sokyu), in an entry referring to this work, states that "in the tokonoma there hung a painting of a duck by Hui Tsung—a female duck." (This scroll comprised two paintings of ducks, one male and the other, re-

34. Yohen temmoku *tea bowl called Inaba Temmoku. Chien ware; diameter, 12 cm. Southern Sung dynasty, thirteenth century. Seikado, Tokyo.*

35. Haikatsugi *(ash glaze)* temmoku *tea bowl. Diameter, 12.8 cm. South-ern Sung dynasty, thirteenth century. Seikado, Tokyo.*

36. Korean kofuki *(powdery) tea bowl called Miyoshi. Diameter, 15.4 cm.*
Yi dynasty, fifteenth or sixteenth century. Mitsui family, Tokyo.

37. *Interior view of Tai-an tearoom, showing east wall. Attributed to Sen no Rikyu. About 1582. Myoki-an temple, Kyoto Prefecture.*

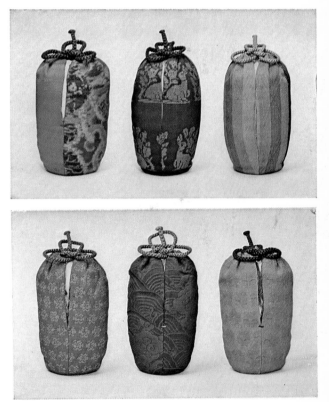

39. *Top: high-shouldered tea caddy called Yari no Saya (Spear Sheath). Old Seto ware; height, 9.4 cm. Sixteenth century. Middle and bottom: six covers for the Yari no Saya.*

38. *Interior view of Zangetsu-tei teahouse, designed by Sen Shoan. Originally built in late sixteenth century; rebuilt in 1909. Omote Senke school of tea, Kyoto. (See also Figure 199.)*

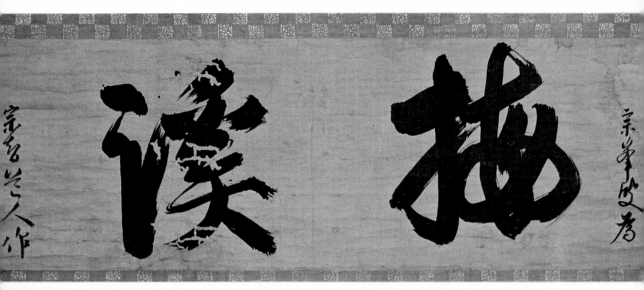

◁ *40 (opposite, top). Calligraphic scroll known as* Plum Valley, *by Daito Kokushi (Shuho Myocho). Ink on cloth; height, 33.3 cm.; width, 99.9 cm. First half of fourteenth century. Goto Art Museum, Tokyo.*

◁ *41 (opposite, bottom). Chinese tea caddy called Fuji Nasu. Height, 5.9 cm. Ming dynasty, fifteenth or sixteenth century. Maeda Ikutoku-kai, Tokyo.*

42 (above). Temple Bell in the Evening Mist, *attributed to Mu-ch'i (Fa-ch'ang). One of a set of eight hand scrolls entitled* Eight Views of the Hsiao and the Hsiang. *Ink on paper; height, 33 cm.; length, 104 cm. Southern Sung dynasty, twelfth or thirteenth century. Hatakeyama Museum, Tokyo.*

43 (right). Square kettle, by Tsuji Yojiro. Iron; height, 21 cm. Sixteenth century. Fujita family, Tokyo.

44, 45. Interior views of En-an teahouse. Above: view showing tokonoma (left) and host's entrance (right). Facing page: view showing server's seat and shikishi windows. Originally designed by Furuta Oribe (1544–1615); rebuilt about 1830–35; relocated in 1867. Yabunouchi school of tea, Kyoto. (See also Figure 198.)

47. White temmoku *tea bowl. Diameter, 13.5 cm. Second half of sixteenth century.*

ferred to here, female.) The celebrated *Dove and Peach Blossoms* (Fig. 32) may in fact be one of the pair referred to as "the *Dove* and *Quail* by Emperor Hui Tsung" in the section of the catalogue listing "small diptychs." Despite its inclusion in the list, however, the latter of the pair has never been traced. Mentioned in the same catalogue, classified under "tetraptychs," are the "landscapes by Emperor Hui Tsung." Three of the four correspond to the scrolls handed down to the Kuon-ji temple in Yamanashi Prefecture and to the Konchi-in subtemple of the Daitoku-ji—namely, the *Summer Landscape, Autumn Landscape,* and *Winter Landscape,* painted at the end of the Northern Sung or the beginning of the Southern Sung dynasty (about 1127)—although they are no longer attributed to Hui Tsung by modern scholars.

There can be no doubt, therefore, that many of the other Chinese paintings handed down to us from this period were once the properties of the Ashikaga shogunate.

Among handicraft art objects, too, a good many are thought to be masterpieces handed down from the Eastern Hills Villa. Most certainly among them are treasures such as the *yohen temmoku* bowls; the *yuteki* (oil spot) *temmoku* bowls dotted with silvery specks on a black glaze (Fig. 15); and the *taihi* (tortoise shell) *san* (Fig. 16), which are *temmoku* bowls with a tortoise-shell pattern on the outer surface. That Japan is known today the world over as a treasury of celadon porcelain may well have resulted precisely from the fact that there did once exist such a period when Chinese objects were bathed in the light of *suki.*

◁ *46. Water jar with landscape design. Shino ware; height, 17.5 cm. Sixteenth century. Yorozuya family, Osaka.*

48. Sweet Flags, *by Po Tzu-t'ing. Ink on silk; height, 116 cm.; width, 60 cm. Yuan dynasty, fourteenth century. Umezawa family, Kanagawa Prefecture.*

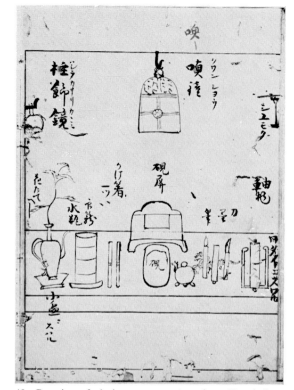

49. *Drawing of* shoin *ornamentation, from* Kundaikan Sa-u Choki *(Catalogue of Ashikaga Yoshimasa's Collection), by Noami. 1566. Tokyo National Museum.*

Transmission of handicraft objects from the end of the Higashiyama period to the middle of the Edo period (1603–1868) is obscure compared with that of paintings. The likely explanation is that, whereas Chinese paintings continued to be accorded the highest esteem at all times, the rise of *wabi* tea caused Chinese vessels like tea bowls, flower containers, and pots to be removed from active use. It seems that even among the Chinese paintings, while the meditational Zen-inspired works such as those by Mu-ch'i and Yu-chien continued to be highly treasured even after the beginning of the Momoyama period, works on other themes were in fact used much less.

The *cha-no-yu* style in vogue under the leadership of Juko, Soju, and Jo-o is regarded as semiformal tea. It was an age that saw the tea ceremony move

in the direction of *wabi,* but unfortunately few records remain to describe the way utensils were actually used at the time. That the use of plain Japanese pottery was on the way to becoming common is suggested by Juko's statement that Bizen wares (of Okayama Prefecture), Ise wares (of Mie Prefecture), and Shigaraki wares (of Shiga Prefecture), if they were attractive and skillfully made, were superior to the expensive Chinese ones. And yet, when one looks at the masterpieces that belonged to Juko and Jo-o, such as those described in the *Matsuya Meibutsu Ki* (Record of Matsuya's Renowned Objects), it would seem evident from their taste for Chinese pictures that they still retained their respect for the tradition of the Eastern Hills Villa, the trend toward *wabi* notwithstanding. Juko owned, among others, the *Snowy Heron*

50. Kare-sansui (dry-landscape) garden. Fourteenth century. Saiho-ji, Kyoto.

by Hsu Hsi, a Later T'ang (923–36) painter famous for his ink paintings of bird-and-flower themes; the *Sweet Flags* (Fig. 48) by Po Tzu-t'ing, a Yuan-dynasty T'ient'ai (Tendai) priest and painter outstanding for his renderings of plants and trees; the diptych *Fruits* by Chao-ch'ang, a Ch'an (Zen) priest and satirical poet of the Sung dynasty; Mu-ch'i's *Returning Sails on a Vast Bay*; and the *Orchids* of Yu-chien. In Jo-o's possession were the *Fruits* inherited from Juko and the *Sunset* by Ma Lin (mid-thirteenth century), son of the celebrated court-style painter of Southern Sung, Ma Yuan (early thirteenth century).

In the case of tea bowls, the taste for *wabi* seems to have shown itself strongly. Of the *temmoku* bowls, Juko did not own a *yohen* or a *yuteki* but a *haikatsugi* (ash glaze) bowl (Fig. 35). This kind of

bowl was not thought much of at the Eastern Hills Villa, yet when arranged in combination with water jars of Bizen and Shigaraki ware it fits much better than the *yuteki* or *yohen* bowls, and here the trend toward *wabi* can clearly be seen taking shape.

Again, the taste of these men is reflected much more vividly in the wares that were not catalogued as *meibutsu*. Among works of Chinese porcelain, for example, Juko's exceedingly subdued Chinese celadon porcelain is a good illustration, while Jo-o had a special attachment to the highly prized products of Seto known as "white *temmo-ku*" tea bowls (Fig. 47), an early type of Shino ware from Mino Province (present Gifu Prefecture) characterized by a crackled white glaze. In 1554, the year before Jo-o's death, there was published the *Chagu Bito Shu*, a listing and explanation

of tea-utensil types by Nanjo Sokin. Catalogued therein are utensils of Seto *temmoku*, the *imogashira* (European-style water jars known for their taro-like shapes), Shigaraki and Bizen wares, and also the Koryo tea bowls of Yi-dynasty (1392–1910) Korea. After Jo-o's time—that is, from the mid-sixteenth century on—the trend toward *wabi* tea increased sharply, centering on the merchants of Sakai, Hakata (in present Fukuoka Prefecture), and Kyoto.

UTENSILS OF INFORMAL TEA In 1564 the *Bunrui Sojimboku* (Classified Facts About Tea), a book on the connoisseurship of tea utensils transcribed by Shinsosai Shunkei and thought possibly to contain the teachings of Jo-o, whose disciple he was, recorded that "the *suki* of today has reached a stage where it allows no room for Chinese wares." Then in 1568, the *Tea Diary of Tsuda Sokyu* made reference to a Mishima tea bowl, a type of Korean bowl with a rope pattern incised with a spatula on the inner and outer surface. From about the 1530s on through the middle of the sixteenth century, Korean tea bowls had been in use under the vague denomination of "Koryo tea bowls." These now began to be clearly classified when listed in the records of tea parties as Mishima and Ido. (The latter, of a rough shape with flaring sides and glazed all over with loquat color, were commonly in use among the Korean peasantry.) This development reveals a growing interest in Korean wares. It was probably about this time, too, that Miyoshi Chokei (1523–64), a retainer of the Ashikaga shogunate's deputy Hosokawa Harumoto (1514–63), gained possession of the *kofuki* (powdery) tea bowl (Fig. 36), an *o-meibutsu* Korean bowl covered with a dull white glaze and marked with a bamboo-leaf-like shape where the glaze was not applied. (*O-meibutsu* are renowned objects dating from before the time of

51. *Tea bowl called Nitoku. Mishima ware; diameter, 14.7 cm. Yi dynasty, fifteenth or sixteenth century. Mitsui family, Tokyo.*

52. *Tea bowl called Oguro, by Tanaka Chojiro. Black Raku ware; diameter, 10.75 cm. Second half of sixteenth century.*

Jo-o and Rikyu.) From the 1570s on, the new men of power, headed by Oda Nobunaga and Toyotomi Hideyoshi, placed great value on Koryo tea bowls and especially on Ido bowls, the most highly prized among these, such as the one called Tsutsuizutsu (Fig. 7). This is a loquat-colored, crackled bowl once presented by Tsutsui Junkei (1549–84) to Hideyoshi. At that time, too, wares reflecting the tastes of tea men like Rikyu and Sokyu began to emerge from the kilns at Seto, Bizen, and Shigaraki.

For Nobunaga and Hideyoshi, however, it was necessary also to possess *meibutsu* from the Eastern Hills Villa as a means of flaunting their authority, and they particularly sought paintings and tea caddies (*cha-ire*) of Chinese origin. On Nobunaga's entry into Kyoto in 1569 he immediately made use of his authority to confiscate such well-known tea caddies as the Matsumoto Nasu, an eggplant-shaped *o-meibutsu* owned at the time by Matsu-

moto Shuho; the Fuji Nasu (Fig. 41), also an *o-meibutsu* and likened to Mount Fuji for its noble shape; and the Hatsuhana (First Flower) Katatsuki, a high-shouldered tea caddy given its name by Ashikaga Yoshimasa on account of its great nobility and beauty. Besides these, Nobunaga owned a collection of scrolls, among them several from the *Eight Views of the Hsiao and the Hsiang* by Mu-ch'i and by Yu-chien. Hideyoshi, following in the footsteps of Nobunaga, devoted himself enthusiastically to the collection of renowned wares, a means by which he hoped to focus attention on his position as absolute ruler of the land.

It was Rikyu's lot to serve as head tea master to Hideyoshi, as we have already noted, and in his tea there appeared two distinct facets: the *cha-no-yu* that reflected the gorgeous life style of his master and the *cha-no-yu* that sought the depths where tea and Zen fused in one single spirit. It was about 1582 that he built the Tai-an tearoom at the Myo-

53. Calligraphy known as Encouragement in Zen, *by Liao-an Ch'ing-yu. Ink on paper; height, 27.9 cm.; length, 73.9 cm. Yuan dynasty, 1341. Tokyo National Museum.*

ki-an temple near Kyoto. Then, beginning in 1586, he commissioned the potter Chojiro (1516–92) to make bowls to suit his own taste, thus bringing to the world of *wabi* tea utensils an aspect not seen in the tea of Juko or Jo-o. Chojiro, it should be noted, was the Kyoto potter who founded the tradition of the soft hand-shaped Raku ware.

The tea bowls of Chojiro are symbolic of Rikyu's tea. Typical among them are the Muichibutsu (Fig. 8), a Red Raku tea bowl later classified by Kobori Enshu (1579–1647) as a *chuko* (rediscovered) *meibutsu,* and the large-sized Black Raku tea bowl called Oguro (Fig. 52), one of Rikyu's favorite *meibutsu.* The air of utter tranquility that conceals within itself the artifice of the potter made these bowls an excellent expression of the spirit of Rikyu's tea, in which Rikyu himself longed for "the true taste of the heart, which is to find taste in nothing itself." In his old age he customarily decorated the tokonoma of his 2-mat or his 4.5-mat tearoom with an example of calligraphy by the famous Chinese Zen abbot Liao-an Ch'ing-yu (Fig. 53) and used his favorite square kettle (Fig. 43) and the Red Raku tea bowl by Chojiro called Ki Mamori. He also used Shigaraki and Seto water jars. He hosted countless tea parties with this ar-

rangement, which represents the full flowering of his *wabi* tea.

"The essence of the *cha-no-yu* lies in the *soan* tea. For the tea of the formal *shoin* and *daisu* the social rules are extremely strict—this is the convention; and while the informal small room and the garden have as their model those formal rules, in the end they part with them and forget all artificial skills so as to enter the world of freedom and find the true taste of the heart, which is to find taste in nothing itself. In doing so, the *soan* tea breaks away from the convention." Rikyu is here stressing the ideal of informal tea. This informal tea had its point of departure in the formal *shoin* tea, where Chinese wares reigned supreme, then passed through the semiformal, and finally attained the informal. The last of these, incorporating Rikyu's taste in the shape of the Tai-an tearoom and the Chojiro tea bowls, represented the consummation of one Japanese concept of aesthetic values.

It is of great interest to note in passing that within this current only the *Eight Views of the Hsiao and the Hsiang* by Mu-ch'i and by Yu-chien have held the spotlight in every age, which suggests that perhaps the world they depict contains more perfectly than any other the true ideal of the *cha-no-yu.*

CHAPTER THREE

Suki: Artistic Taste

THE TENSHO ERA (1573–92), that interval of the Momoyama period in which Rikyu was destined to flourish, witnessed the whole country united under one centralized rule but still suffering the damaging effects of the long internal wars that had ravaged it. Rikyu experienced strong feelings of antipathy toward his authoritarian master, Hideyoshi. But as his spiritual support, he maintained his loyalty to the former lord of Sakai, Miyoshi Chokei, and selected for his own grave a site in the latter's family temple, the Juko-in, a subtemple of the Daitoku-ji in Kyoto. Thus Rikyu manifestly practiced in his own life the feudal morality of the master-retainer relationship.

ORIBE'S TASTE FOR IRREGULARITY After Rikyu's death, Hideyoshi was apparently overcome with profound sorrow and never appointed another tea master to replace him. Yet one man did in fact take over Rikyu's role, coming strongly to the fore after Hideyoshi's death in 1598 and achieving even greater prominence after the Battle of Sekigahara two years later. This man was none other than Furuta Oribe (1544–1615). Younger than Rikyu by more than twenty years, he experienced the reality of war as a military commander, and his life was in tune with the times in which he lived. It was Oribe who first introduced the concept of play into the tea world and by that move alone brought it much closer to the lives of common people. In general it

may be said that Oribe, in contrast with the ethical Rikyu, was undoubtedly a pleasure-loving man.

Oribe learned from Rikyu the creative ingenuity required to make historical tradition serve a new creation and also the manner of providing an outlet for fresh feelings in a world tightly bound by tradition. Rikyu, instead of leaning toward Chinese wares, had directed his attention to local pottery such as came from Ise and Bizen. In like manner, Oribe made positive efforts to adopt the *namban* designs. *Namban*—literally, "southern barbarians" —was a term applied to Europeans who reached Japan from Spain and Portugal by way of the south in the sixteenth century and, through their manners and customs, inspired a unique genre of Japanese art.

Oribe was the first tea instructor of the second Tokugawa shogun, Hidetada (1579–1632), and rose to occupy the highest position in the *cha-no-yu* world of his day. A passage from the *Sojimboku*, a book on the manners and methods of the *cha-no-yu* published in 1612 by an unknown author, describes how Oribe's taste tended toward the asymmetric: "Every year, new asymmetric tea bowls baked in Seto were sent to him in Kyoto, as were also other bowls produced in the same year." Sotan, too, recorded in his diary that at Oribe's morning tea party on February 28, 1599, of the lunar calendar, Oribe used an odd-shaped, asymmetrical tea bowl from Seto. This discovery of beauty in irregular shapes was in fact not unrelated to the

54. *Letter written by Sen no Rikyu to his disciple Matsui Yasuyuki. Ink on paper. 1591. Matsui family, Kumamoto Prefecture.*

new feeling awakening in the society of his day. The asymmetry in round forms accords with the "leaning" (*kabuku*) of upright forms. Such a leaning posture symbolized at the time the mentality of self-indulgence (*kabuki*), which was never to be found in Rikyu but which Oribe did possess.

The Battle of Sekigahara (1600), which signified a victory for Tokugawa Ieyasu (1542–1616) over the army of Hideyoshi's ally Ishida Mitsunari (1560–1600), also marked the last moments of Rikyu's world and the birth of Oribe's. As in the political sphere, this was a decisive turning point in the history of *chado*, the way of tea, for it was at this time that the tea ceremony of modern times made a start and the idolization of Rikyu got under way. Fifteen years later, Osaka Castle, the stronghold of Hideyoshi's son Hideyori (1593–1615), fell to the Tokugawa forces after the Winter Siege of 1614–15 and the Summer Siege of 1615, and Ieyasu's mastery of Japan was virtually complete. The circumstances forced many people to take a clear stand in their alliances, Oribe among them. Accused by the followers of Ieyasu of treason against the shogun, he was ordered to die by sep-

puku and had all his possessions confiscated. Like Rikyu before him, he faced his end with a good grace, making no attempt to defend himself.

A point meriting some attention at this stage is the stand adopted by two men deeply involved with the tea cult. One of them was Kanamori Sowa (1584–1656), of whom we shall have occasion to hear more later. On the day set for the march to the Winter Siege of Osaka Castle, his father, Kanamori Arishige, lord of Takayama Castle in Hida Province (present Gifu Prefecture), hurried with many other retainers to join the Eastern Army commanded by Tokugawa Ieyasu. Despite being heir to his father, Sowa turned his back on him and, after renouncing his samurai rank, made his way up to Kyoto. The other man, of great renown as a samurai in Mikawa Province (present Aichi Prefecture), was Ishikawa Jozan (1583–1672). He felt dissatisfied at being treated as socially inferior despite his position as *fudai*, or vassal of the Tokugawa, since before the Battle of Sekigahara. He rushed out ahead of other vassals on the battlefield, thus disobeying orders. Then, like Sowa, he renounced his rank of samurai. Later

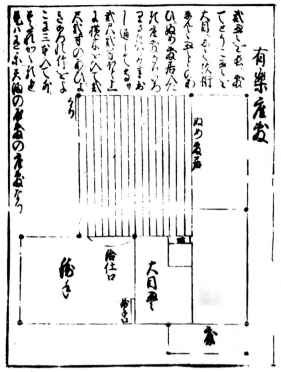

55. *Plan of a tearoom designed by Oda Uraku. From* Sukiya Kuho Shu *(On Building Teahouses), by Ito Kageharu. 1686.*

punished for this action, he led a life of forced seclusion in the Shisen-do, his retreat on Mount Hiei near Kyoto, and there began his career of artistic refinement (*furyu*). In this way, the *cha-no-yu* also fulfilled the function of providing, in the *soan*, a place of refuge for men who sought an escape from the heavy pressures of feudal society.

KOETSU'S SPIRIT OF RESISTANCE Oribe's disciples included many samurai and merchants, of whom one of the best known was Hon'ami Koetsu (1556–1637). Koetsu's family were descendants of the *doboshu* Hon'ami, who, as an attendant at the court of the first Ashikaga shogun, Takauji (1305–58), worked as a sword cleaner and polisher. Koetsu's great-grandfather, Honko, had married into the

Hon'ami family from the Matsuda family, stout adherents of the Hokke (Lotus) sect of Buddhism in Bizen. After Honko's entry into the Hon'ami family, its members also became followers of Hokke Buddhism, and Honko himself successively inherited the family's three professions: sword cleaning, sword polishing, and connoisseurship. Honko's son, Koshin, had no children; so he adopted a son, Koji, from the family of Kataoka Tsugidayu, Honko's younger brother-in-law. Koetsu was Koji's eldest son. Later a son named Kosatsu was born to Koshin. Koetsu married Kosatsu's daughter and thus had a certain amount of freedom to pursue various artistic activities outside the bounds of the family business. Yet, while his father, Koji, was still alive, Koetsu helped him in his work. One of the tasks entrusted to him was to handle business

56. *Cover of Kanze-school Noh-play text in Saga-bon edition. Early seventeenth century.*

with the Maeda clan of Kaga Province (present Ishikawa Prefecture), from whom Koji had received a fief. It was only after Koji's death in 1603 that Koetsu gave full play to his abilities. His occupations included the publication, in cooperation with his disciple Suminokura Soan (1570–1632), of the Saga-bon, or Saga editions (Fig. 56), block-printed works of Japanese literature published at Saga in Kyoto. After the Summer Siege of 1615 he took up residence in the famous district Takagamine (Fig. 57), northwest of Kyoto. If this event is viewed in connection with Oribe's forced seppuku, then Tokugawa Ieyasu's policy of granting Koetsu land at Takagamine appears to have been a double-edged one: it served the purpose of providing a show of generosity toward Koetsu and, at the same time, of conveniently banishing him from Kyoto. It would seem that such a course of action was suggested to Ieyasu by his vassal Itakura Katsushige (1545–1626). As the rich merchant Haiya Shoeki (1610–91), known for his *chado* and his calligraphy, pointed out, "throughout his life Koetsu shunned all worldly wisdom in his way of living" by refusing to admit the existence of the feudal system and to submit to its authority. Openly declaring his "aversion to catering to the tastes of those in power," he disregarded them and went happily about his pottery, writing, and painting. From this point of view, it is inconceivable that he would have let himself be swayed from the path of his convictions by the mere gift of land at Takagamine, for his heart was full of the vigorous spirit of resistance of a Hokke believer who was at the same time a townsman of the old capital, Kyoto. It was this spirit of resistance that lay at the heart of the beauty he created. Though he lived as a recluse, his works never lost their clarity, and he exhibited throughout his life an attitude of pride and dignity.

Koetsu and his relative Tawaraya Sotatsu, a

57. *View of Takagamine, Kyoto, where Hon'ami Koetsu was granted land by Tokugawa Ieyasu and established a community of artists and craftsmen.*

famous painter of the early Edo period and a collaborator in the publishing of the Saga-bon, belonged to the class of men—we may call them Kyoto's upper-class *machishu* (townspeople)—who, on account of their opposition to the Tokugawa shogunate, were in close connection with the court of Emperor Gomizuno-o (1596–1680; r. 1611–29) and gave their support to the Kan'ei culture, so called after the era of the same name (1624–44). This culture marked a return to the classics, not to be seen in Edo, the town of shogun and samurai. Its tradition reached into the house of Ogata Sohaku, of the same group as Koetsu and thought to have been related to him, who lived with him in Takagamine. In due course Sohaku's house witnessed the birth of two grandsons, both destined to become famous—namely, the painter Korin (1658–1716) and the ceramist Kenzan (1663–1743). Their art, like that of Koetsu, had its roots in classicism, but it surmounted this stage and, in

so doing, attained its true value. There is no doubt, however, that this art achieved a great significance because of the heritage Koetsu left them.

In the artistic tradition of the Momoyama period, stretching from Oribe to Koetsu, and then to Korin and Kenzan, we can follow the trail of the most superb cultural creation Japan has known, at once the quintessence of *furyu* (aesthetic refinement) and the true expression of *suki*, which we have already defined as artistic taste, but which also implies a love of refined art. It was supported by the privileged merchants known as upper-class *machishu*, and it heralded the prosperous heyday of the townsmen's world.

The true meaning of *suki* was contained in the way of tea that developed after Rikyu's time. The term was already in use in earlier times to denote a man who possessed tea utensils. The following mention of it is made in the *Shotetsu Monogatari* (Tale of Shotetsu), a study of Japanese poetry pub-

58. *Tea bowl with notched foot. Diameter, 11.8 cm. Yi dynasty, sixteenth century. Hatakeyama Museum, Tokyo.*

lished by the poet-priest Shotetsu (1381–1459) in 1430: "There are many forms of *suki* in poetry and likewise many in the *cha-no-yu*. In tea, *suki* means first of all taking care of the tea utensils. He who seeks as best he can to treasure his collection of *kensan* [from the Chien-ming kilns in Fukien] and *temmoku* bowls, his tea whisks and water jars, deserves to be called a 'man of *suki* in tea' [*cha no sukisha*]." Shotetsu then attempts, by comparing the tea utensils, to discern the difference between a *sukisha* and a *chakurai* or *chanomi*. The *chakurai* (tea taster) could distinguish the good and bad teas by their taste, and the *chanomi* (tea drinker) drank in quantity from a large tea bowl with no discernment of the quality of the tea. The tea utensils referred to above are, of course, wares from China. Yet, though the *suki* of tea was interpreted in this way at the time, the term in fact means more than just the possession of tea utensils. It also means

taking good care of them, as suggested by the original meaning of the term *cha suki*, "the love of tea," and finding pleasure in arranging them. Such a trend was reflected, for example, in Soju's being called at the time the "leader of *suki*." Though *suki* was an attribute of all the tea masters, the word acquired a new depth of meaning with the advent of the Momoyama period. The *Sumpu Ki*, a diary in which Goto Mitsutsugu (1571–1625) chronicled the happenings in Sumpu (present city of Shizuoka) during the period 1611–15, notes on August 14, 1612, of the lunar calendar, that "Oribe is a master of *suki* in our time. This *suki* is greatly respected by the shogun [Ieyasu], and many samurai who practice the *daimyo cha* do so both morning and night." Such a statement was possible because of the imitation of their superiors by low-ranking samurai and the arrival at a stage in *suki* where enjoyment had given way to indulgence.

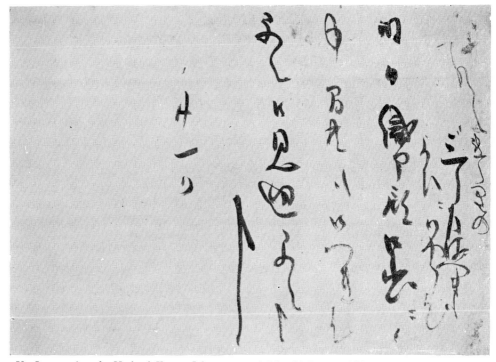

59. Letter written by Hon'ami Koetsu. Ink on paper; height, 28.6 cm.; width, 41.4 cm. Late sixteenth or early seventeenth century. Mino family, Kanagawa Prefecture.

SANSAI, THE CONSERVATIVE

Shortly before his death, Rikyu was ordered by an irate Hideyoshi to confine himself in his residence in Sakai. From Kyoto to Sakai he was to travel by boat on the Yodo River. On the day of his departure, only two men braved Hideyoshi's anger to bid their master a sad farewell at the landing place in Fushimi, Kyoto. Oribe was one, and the other was Rikyu's young disciple at the time, Hosokawa Tadaoki (1563–1645), also known by his priest name of Sansai. Sansai was nineteen years younger than Oribe, and in fact the three men— Rikyu, Oribe, and Sansai—can be compared to father, son, and grandson. Sansai lacked Oribe's creative flair, but by loyally following Rikyu and giving generous welcome to Oribe's ideas he lived successfully through this age of *suki*. From his father, Yusai (Hosokawa Fujitaka; 1534–1610), he received a classical education. His marriage to

Tamako (1564–1600), second daughter of Akechi Mitsuhide (1526–82) and better known to the Western world by her Christian name Gracia, also brought him into contact with a Christian environment. This in turn helped him establish a good relationship with Oribe, himself deeply interested in Christianity. Sansai's life was that of an outstanding conservative, which explains why his name, along with that of Gamo Ujisato (1556–95), was never once omitted from any list of Rikyu's "Seven Talented Disciples." Here he stands in strong contrast with Oribe. Originally included in the same list, Oribe was eventually dropped.

It was in Sansai's time that books concerning tea began to be published, in anticipation of the full flowering of the way of tea. Concerning the *Nambo Roku*, doubts yet remain as to when it was completed. Oribe's *Oribe Hyakkajo* (Oribe's Hundred Rules), containing the rules of tea he inherited

from Rikyu, and *Furuta Oribe Densho* (Writings of
Furuta Oribe) were disseminated around the 1630s,
and in 1641 the *Hosokawa Cha-no-yu Sho* (Hosokawa's Book of the Tea Ceremony) by Sansai, containing the hundred rules of Rikyu as listed by
Oribe, was transcribed. These works, together with
the *Sojimboku* and others, are known to have been
published from about the 1660s. Sansai wrote of
both Rikyu and Oribe, but he did it without sur-
rendering his own ego. In a statement like "I, Lord
Tadaoki, detest seeing the lid of the kettle removed
before the water has begun to boil," his use of the
expression "I, Lord Tadaoki" reminds one vividly
of the figure of a true daimyo.

THE EXPANSION OF
THE TEAROOM

Both the 4.5-mat tea-
room and the 2-mat tea-
room in Rikyu's Juraku
residence, built when he was at the peak of his
career, featured low ceilings (less than 2 meters),
controlled light, and extremely taut spatial composition, thereby expressing a profound spiritual
search for ultimate truth. Rikyu reduced the size
of the *koma* (tearoom of less than 4.5-mat size) to
1.5 mats, lowered the ceiling of the tokonoma considerably—as, for example, in the Tai-an tearoom
(5.2 *shaku*, or about 1.57 meters)—and cut down
the size of the entrance to the smallest limit, re-
stricting the use of each part and the behavior of
the people in the room from every angle. With all
this he strove to attain perfection for the *soan* style
of tea. The tearoom, in that truth-seeking expression transcending the conditions of everyday life,
can be said to have created a standard of its own.

The *soan*-style tearoom, which owes its perfection
chiefly to Rikyu, exerted a widespread influence.
This, however, did not consist simply of imitation
by numerous people. It was, rather, that influential

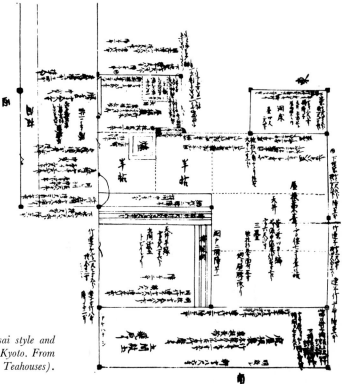

61. *Plan of a teahouse built in the Hosokawa Sansai style and located at the Shinjo-in subtemple of the Tenryu-ji, Kyoto. From* Juhachi Kakoi no Zu *(Drawings of Eighteen Teahouses). National Diet Library, Tokyo.*

tea men based themselves on its standards to produce original styles of their own. A case in point is that of Oda Uraku (1547–1621), younger brother of the daimyo Oda Nobunaga. He was born into a noble family from Owari Province (present Aichi Prefecture). He admired Jo-o and took lessons from Rikyu. His position as a tea master was, however, of a rather special character. He was equipped with the knowledge to direct the decorating of the shogunal reception room (*onari shoin*) in the mansion of Maeda Toshiie (1538–99), had a great gift for interior design, and revealed a style that was both original and spectacular.

The Jo-an tearoom at the Shoden-in subtemple of the Kennin-ji (Figs. 30, 70), built in his late years and now preserved at the Shiroyama Villa of the Mitsui family in Kanagawa Prefecture, drew widespread attention at the time on account of its diagonal wall at one side of the tokonoma, which

earned it the appellation *sujichigai no kakoi* (oblique enclosure), and its peculiar style of central post (*naka-bashira*). His design coupled the clarity of the warrior with the aristocracy of the nobleman. His tearoom in Nijo Castle in Kyoto and another in the Temma mansion in Osaka contain many other examples of his work. Typical is his attaching a wide, wooden-floored veranda to create the illusion that the room is a step higher. In doing so, he tried to distinguish clearly the main guest's seat from those of the other participants. This device was totally absent from Rikyu's tearooms, where great stress was laid on the equality of all the guests.

Hosokawa Sansai was the conservative successor to Rikyu's style, even in the tearoom. Fond of the *murodoko* (clay-walled tokonoma) style of *wabi* structure, he loyally followed the spirit of Rikyu, at the same time making free use of the various forms and

62. View of Ko-an teahouse. Originally built in late eighteenth century; relocated about 1908. Sangen-in, Daitoku-ji, Kyoto.

techniques found in the *soan*. His loyalty to Rikyu notwithstanding, he did not neglect the needs of his time and instituted a new trend that would match the feelings and usage of the warriors. In contrast with Sansai, Furuta Oribe paid great heed to the entertainment of the nobles and in doing so gave a great impetus to a style of tearoom really suited to samurai society. It is said of him that "on the visit of the shogun, the use of a 2-plus-a-*daime*-mat room [a *daime* being a three-quarter mat] placed the host too close to the guest of honor, which situation he remedied by converting the room to a 3-plus-a-*daime*-mat room." In this way he enlarged the standard of the small tearoom and conceived a device to determine the seats of the remaining participants. Most typical of his style is the En-an teahouse (Figs. 10, 44, 45, 77–80, 182, 183), located in the Shimogyo district of Kyoto and handed down in the Yabunouchi family. A 3-mat guest seat is placed between the host's *daime*

mat (server's seat) and the seats for the other participants, the outstanding feature here being a double sliding panel (*fusuma*) separating the main guest's seat from those of the other participants. On the basis of this double *fusuma* and the remaining mats, several styles of use were conceivable, and it was likewise possible to expand or reduce the area of the guests' seats. This En-an style of tearoom received the wholehearted support of the samurai and enjoyed a time of great popularity.

In this way Rikyu's successors began to develop the device of "handling the *soan*-style room in just the same way as the *shoin*," as we read in the *Nambo Roku*. Soon they were pressing even further. The *Chado Oda Uraku Densho* (Writings of Oda Uraku on Tea) says that "2.5-mat rooms and 1.5-mat rooms are uncomfortable for the guests." Not much time had passed before they were demanding a relaxation of the "truth-seeking" approach to tea.

Since Muromachi times it had been customary

63. *Tea bowl called Furuta Korai. Goshomaru ware (after Oribe's design); diameter, 13 cm. Yi dynasty, sixteenth or seventeenth century.*

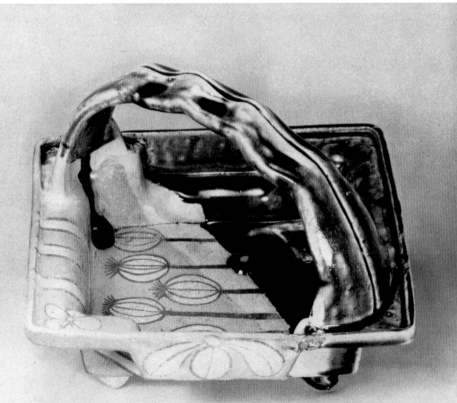

64. *Square dish with handle. Oribe ware; diameter, 21.4 cm. Sixteenth century.*

65. *Section of* Waka Makimono. *Poetry scroll with calligraphy by Hon'ami Koetsu over paintings of grasses and flowers of the four seasons attributed to Tawaraya Sotatsu.*

66. *Tea bowl called Seppo (Snow-covered Peak), by Hon'ami Koetsu. Red Raku ware; diameter, 10.9 cm. First half of seven-*

67. *Tea bowl called Otogoze (Homely Woman), by Hon'ami Koetsu. Red Raku ware; diameter, 11.5 cm. First half of seven-*

山のいなつて
いけて
月

おもり
の庭の

ぬ
ておもり
物と

たち庵
む

ぬ
も

Ink and colors on paper; dimensions of entire scroll: height, 33.7 cm.; length, 924.1
cm. First half of seventeenth century. Hatakeyama Museum, Tokyo.

68. Tea bowl called Shigure (Autumn Rain), by Hon'ami
Koetsu. Black Raku ware; diameter, 12.5 cm. First half of
seventeenth century. Morikawa family, Aichi Prefecture.

69. Tea bowl called Fujisan (Mount Fuji), by Hon'ami Koetsu. White Raku ware; diameter, 11.6 cm. First half of seventeenth century. Sakai family, Tokyo. (See also Figure 12.)

71. *Outer veranda of Bosen tearoom, designed by Kobori Enshu. Originally built about 1644; rebuilt in 1797. Koho-an, Daitoku-ji, Kyoto.*

◁ 70. *Exterior view of Jo-an teahouse, designed by Oda Uraku. About 1618. Shiroyama Villa, Mitsui family, Kanagawa Prefecture.*

73. Interior view of Yu-in tearoom, showing server's seat. Designed by Sen Sotan; originally built about 1653; rebuilt in late eighteenth century. Ura Senke school of tea, Kyoto.

◁ *72. Interior view of Sa-an tearoom, designed by Konoike Ryoei. About 1742. Gyokurin-in, Daitoku-ji, Kyoto.*

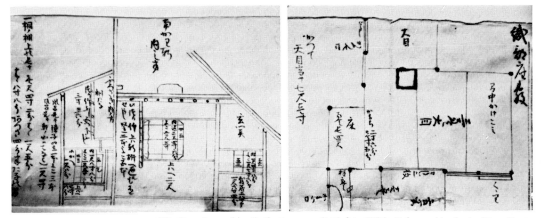

75. Drawings of an Oribe tearoom. Copied in 1738. Yabunouchi school of tea, Kyoto.

to meet in another room for a banquet before or after the *cha-no-yu*. From the 1580s on, this custom became so tremendously popular that a *shoin* or a hall (*hiroma*; literally, "large room") came to be required for any tea party. A glance at the menus contained in the records of tea parties of the time brings home vividly the scale of these banquets, and the fact that the *Hideyoshi Shoin Furumai Satagaki* (Hideyoshi's Instructions Governing the Banquet in the Shoin) was issued in 1592 is an eloquent witness to their popularity. For Rikyu, trends expressing the belief that it was "impolite not to have a banquet in the 4.5-mat room or in the *shoin* after finishing the *cha-no-yu* in the small room" were a source of uneasiness.

In the meantime a type of room called the *kusari no ma*, or chain room, developed. It adjoined the tearoom and took its name from the chain suspended from the ceiling, to which a kettle was attached. In the actual tea-party records, it is not until the late 1590s that the *kusari no ma* makes its appearance, but in the *Nambo Roku* it is already recorded that it was created by "the councilor of Bizen and Lord Asano, after consultation with Tsuda Sokyu." Faced with this tendency always to meet for a banquet in the *kusari no ma* after the

cha-no-yu, Rikyu issued a severe criticism, pointing out that "the custom of always taking a meal, if continued, . . . will cause the decline of the *wabi cha-no-yu* in later ages." His view was that "even on the occasion of a shogunal visit" the *cha-no-yu* should be held "either in the small tearoom or in the *shoin* —one or the other" and that one must not indulge in the "luxurious practice of changing rooms." In particular, he strongly cautioned against "devising elaborate banquets in the *wabi* room."

It was Oribe who introduced the *kusari no ma* in full scale at tea parties. At the tea party on the lunar February 1, 1604, the guests partook of a tea-ceremony meal (*kaiseki*) and drank *koicha* (thick tea), after which they went out of the room through the host's doorway into the *kusari no ma*. There they hung a kettle from the ceiling and set up *fukuro-dana*, or "pocket shelves," on which were laid out all the utensils required for the *cha-no-yu*. The presence of a *tsuke shoin*, or broad-silled window, made the *kusari no ma* a *shoin*-style room, and here Oribe served *usucha* (light tea) and conversed at leisure with his guests. The *kusari no ma* was usually based on the formula of the *fukuro-dana* and the hanging kettle and, according to the *Hizo Denshin*, the Sansai-school tea book of the eighteenth century,

◁ 74. *Roof of Chosei-an teahouse. Originally built in eighteenth century; rebuilt in 1869. Horinouchi family, Kyoto.*

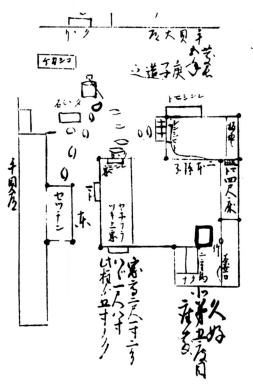

76. Plan of teahouse in Oribe style at residence of Matsuya Hisayoshi. From the Todai-ji version of Cha-no-yu Hisho *(Tea Ceremony Secrets).*

77 (opposite page, left). Tsukubai *(low stone basin) and lantern in garden of En-an teahouse. About 1640–55. Yabunouchi school of tea, Kyoto.*

78 (opposite page, right). Stone-paved walk *with* tatami ishi *(flat embedded stone) in garden of En-an teahouse. About 1640–55. Yabunouchi school of tea, Kyoto.*

represented a phase "midway between the small tearoom and the *shoin.*"

Oribe stressed the importance of adornments in the *kusari no ma*, pointing out that "if there are hanging scrolls and flowers in the tearoom, there should also be some in the *kusari no ma.*" In the *soan*, the space available for ornamentation was extremely limited and ultimately became concentrated entirely in the tokonoma. Until that time, the daimyo, who by their own nature wished to show off the wares in their possession, had found it very difficult to do so in the *soan* room—hence their desire to increase the number of places where tea parties could be held. One solution to their problem was the *kusari no ma*. By combining the tearoom and the *kusari no ma* it became possible to submit any number of tea utensils to the appreciation of the guests, and, as a further effect, the cramped tea ceremony in the small room acquired a feeling of expansion. And again, by joining together the tearoom, *kusari no ma*, and *shoin*, it became possible to have three different kinds of tea, represented by the *soan, fukuro-dana,* and *daisu,* respectively.

The development of the *kusari no ma* progressed parallel to the spread of the small *soan* tearoom. The *soan* room, Rikyu's crystallization of the true meaning of tea, was definitely incorporated in the *daimyo cha*, but its effect was, ironically, to foster the transformation of the tea ceremony into the "luxurious practice of changing rooms."

THE INTRODUCTION OF SCENIC ELEMENTS

Old tradition has it that the stepping-stones in the garden path were for Rikyu "sixty percent path and forty percent view," whereas for Oribe they were "forty percent path and sixty percent view."

The observation is a keen one, because the contrast reflects the different attitudes of the two grand tea masters with regard to garden design.

Rikyu never made a display of his craftsmanship but concealed it deep within, aiming always for a design conducive to deep thought and contemplation. This characteristic of his emerges particularly clearly in the arrangement of the steppingstones under the lean-to of the Tai-an tearoom (Fig. 26) and in the composition of the inner surface of the east wall (Fig. 37). Also, when the window in the west wall of the anteroom in the Tai-an is viewed as it originally was (see Foldout 3), it becomes apparent that its location was determined in conformity with its function. Rikyu never emphasized the expression of independent parts. His aim was to effect an overall spatial composition in which each part played up the unity of the whole. In this respect his sense of "pattern" was weak.

In contrast, Oribe attached importance to the effectiveness of the pattern. We may admit this even when comparing the *tatami ishi* (flat embedded stones) at Rikyu's Tai-an, where small round stones are arranged quite naturally, and the design of the *tatami ishi* in the garden path of Oribe's En-an teahouse (Fig. 78), with accompanying hewn stones inserted in a pattern along the edge. The *shikishi mado* (Fig. 45), two paper windows placed slightly off center one above the other, are thought to have been originated by Oribe, who refers to them as follows in the *Oribe Kikigaki*, notes on his teachings made by an unknown disciple: "The *shikishi mado* are meant not only for light but also to create a view within the room." The windows, in other words, rather than serve merely as a means of illumination, are intended to produce a visual effect. Regarding the "calligraphy window" (*bokuseki mado*), known also as the tokonoma window

79. *View of En-an teahouse, showing* nijiri-guchi. *Originally designed by Furuta Oribe (1544–1615); rebuilt about 1830–35; relocated in 1867. Yabunouchi school of tea, Kyoto.*

80. *Interior view of En-an teahouse, showing shelves in* katte *(kitchen). Originally designed by Furuta Oribe (1544–1615); rebuilt about 1830–35; relocated in 1867. Yabunouchi school of tea, Kyoto.*

and placed in the side wall of the alcove to light the hanging scroll, he said that it was meant "to allow light to fall directly within the tokonoma," thus pointing out its function first, but did not fail to add that it served also "to bring out the best in the flowers ornamenting the tokonoma." Fixing a nail into the lattice of the calligraphy window, he hung from it a container with flowers and in doing so created a new scenic effect within the room. To achieve this, he went so far as to transfer the paper window, normally covering the inside of the opening in the wall, to the outside of it, thus showing off the lattice on the inside, the reverse of the original use.

In the En-an style of tearoom, Oribe made use of a black-lacquered tokonoma-frame base (*shin-nuri kamachi*), and for the jamb on one side of the

host's entrance he employed bamboo. The above are explained in the *Cha-no-yu Hisho*: "If bamboo is used for the jamb, then only a black-lacquered base is suitable for the tokonoma frame." This reveals how carefully Oribe planned the arrangement of the materials for each part of the limited space on the wall that contains the tokonoma and the host's entrance. We see here his concept of composing a space by the combination of several patterns of design. As a result, the spatial tension was somewhat relaxed, and the visual effect was allowed ample freedom to unfold.

At his mansion in the Horikawa section of Kyoto, Oribe cut a skylight type of window in the eaves over the earth-floored entrance to the 3-plus-a-daime-mat tearoom in order to permit a view of Mount Atago, northwest of the city. Thus, as we

81. Interior view of Hasso-an teahouse. Early seventeenth century. Nara National Museum.

can surmise from existing records, he probably brought the total number of windows in the tearoom to eleven. This fondness for numerous windows constituted an important new trend and was also evident in the Shunso-ro teahouse, said to have been built in the Uraku style and originally known as the Kyuso-tei, or Nine-Windowed Pavilion. It merits some attention, too, that by providing windows to permit views of the outdoors Oribe was gradually increasing the role of the "play" element in the tea ceremony—a trend, just setting in at the time, toward a lighter appreciation of beauty.

Oribe also undertook many innovations in the *roji*, the gardenlike approach to the teahouse. One of these, inspired by consideration for the nobility, was to devise new means for enhancing the attractiveness of the approach. He introduced new varie-

ties of plants and included a *sodesuri no matsu*, or sleeve-brushing pine tree. Oribe thus did much to enrich the beauty of the approach to the teahouse. Particularly noteworthy is his use of numerous stone lanterns of his own design. The Oribe-style lantern, whose post rises directly from the ground and has no formal base, is wholly suited to the tea garden, which hitherto had been simply a path and, from Oribe's day, began to take on the appearance of a genuine garden.

ORIBE'S TASTE IN TEA UTENSILS   In his *Chaki Meibutsu Shu* (Collection of Renowned Tea Utensils), written in 1588, Yamanoue Soji, Rikyu's most outstanding disciple, observes that "the age of Hideyoshi and Rikyu witnessed the decline of Chinese tea bowls

82. Tea bowl called Fuyu no Yo (Winter Night). Seto ware of Black Raku type; diameter, 10 cm. Late sixteenth century.

83. Tea bowl. Black Oribe ▷ ware; diameter, 13.8 cm. Second half of sixteenth century.

such as the *temmoku* bowls, and now the Koryo [Ido], Seto, contemporary [Raku], and other bowls may be used as utensils for the *cha-no-yu* as long as their shape is good." These words deserve careful attention in that they convey a very clear picture of the state of the tea world toward the end of the sixteenth century. It emerges as a world in which Chojiro's tea bowls of Soeki shape (so named because they were inspired by Rikyu) shared the limelight with Seto and Koryo bowls as the utensils of the age. Moreover, Soji's statement that practically any utensils may be used for tea "as long as their shape is good"—that is to say, one should indulge in the pursuit of *furyu* without getting entangled in formalities—reveals a striking characteristic of the spirit underlying the approach to tea in Momoyama days.

Yet these same words of Soji's suggest that beneath his efforts to act with freedom of spirit the consciousness of another style—a severely formal one—was still very active. The reason for this is that he reflected limpidly the spirit of Rikyu, who attained the informal style of tea on the basis of the severely standardized formal style embodied in the *daisu* tea in a *shoin* setting. But in the case of Furuta Oribe, who assumed the leadership in the *cha-no-yu* after Rikyu and Soji, there is hardly a trace of consciousness or concern for past styles of tea. Oribe's pursuit of *furyu* was not characterized by an earnest search for truth, as was the goal-oriented Rikyu's, but tended instead to be considerably more free, more active, and more materialistic.

The designs of tea utensils at the time, too, mirror in their willfulness the lively sentiments of an age that lived in the belief that "the time of Miroku [Maitreya] has indeed come," as Miura Joshin expresses it in his *Keicho Kembun Shu* (Collection of Things Seen and Heard in the Keicho Era).

The substance of this belief can be analyzed in three elements. First, it did not coincide with the popular belief that the Bodhisattva Miroku would come to save mankind countless ages after the death of the Buddha but was rather the manifestation of a deeply realistic joy resulting from the peace brought to the land by Hideyoshi after long years of domestic warfare. Second, the idea of the people concerning the "time of Miroku" was, in short, that of a golden age emerging from the development of various industries and the prosperity of Kyoto and Sakai. Third, the "time of Miroku" was expected to coincide with the appearance of many visible novelties, and such novelties could in fact be seen in the *namban* goods and in such undertakings as Hideyoshi's construction of the donjon of Osaka Castle.

Many of the tea bowls preferred by Rikyu, such as Chojiro's bowls of Soeki shape, show strong em-phasis on a spirituality that conceals within itself the artifice of the designer, whereas a great number of the bowls that we can consider as representing Oribe's preferences display the open expression of his own creative intentions.

In his *Sotan Nikki* (Diary of Sotan), Kamiya Sotan (1553–1635), a wealthy merchant of Hakata, mentions that Oribe used Seto tea bowls of warped shape. This type of bowl, known as *kutsugata* (shoe shape) because of its oval mouth and its general form (Fig. 83)—and described in its time as being "funny-shaped"—was a characteristic expression of the new kind of ceramic art introduced by Oribe. Such bowls, of course, were quite different from the Chojiro bowls favored by Rikyu. When one of Chojiro's Soeki-shape bowls and a *kutsugata* bowl are placed side by side, their sharply contrasting character becomes evident, and we see, as it were, a contrast between stillness and movement.

A similar contrast exists in the case of Koryo tea bowls. On the one hand there were the plain, uncontrived styles preferred in Rikyu's day; on the other, those admired and used by Oribe, all of which, like the *kutsugata* bowls, strongly suggested the creative artifice underlying their design. Among the Korean bowls favored in Rikyu's time were the Ido, Mishima, and *kofuki* wares mentioned earlier, as well as the Totoya wares: reddish-brown tea bowls of a rough but quiet taste. Oribe's preferences included the *hori-hakeme* bowls, bearing an incised design resembling brushwork; the *wari-kodai* (split-foot) bowls, with V- or U-shaped notches cut in the foot (Fig. 58); and the white- or gray-glazed *gosho-maru* bowls, the oldest among those made in Korea on the basis of paper models sent from Japan.

This contrast in tastes was not limited to tea bowls. It was also evident in the choice of water jars, flower containers, and, in fact, all other tea-ceremony utensils. The water jars that Rikyu finally chose as the most suitable to match the Chojiro tea bowls were the quietly simple ones of Shigaraki ware. Oribe, on the other hand, preferred to use water jars of exaggeratedly dynamic feeling and boldly warped shape like those of Iga, Bizen, and Shino ware (Figs. 46, 85). The same contrast is to be seen in the choice of the hanging scroll for the tokonoma. Although both men used calligraphic scrolls for this purpose, Rikyu had a special liking for the calligraphy of the Yuan-dynasty Zen abbot Liao-an Ch'ing-yu, while Oribe preferred works of a dynamic character like those of I-shan I-ning (1247–1317), a Southern Sung painter well known for his cursive style of writing (Fig. 84).

Another point of difference between the two tea masters involved the conduct of the tea gathering itself. Rikyu insisted strongly that the ceremony be held from start to finish in the *koma*, or "small room." Oribe, however, made use of the *kusari no ma* as a place for entertaining with light tea, food, and sakè after the drinking of thick tea in the adjoining *koma*. The plates and bowls used on such occasions were highly colorful ones of Oribe, Yellow Seto, and Shino ware. In total contrast with the Zen-inspired *kaiseki* meal favored by Rikyu, these entertainments represented a pleasure-seeking *suki* style, and one of their most notable features was a strong new consciousness of the ornamental value of tea utensils.

From the time of Rikyu's death in 1591 until the end of the Keicho era in 1615, the Oribe taste consistently maintained itself as the free expression of creative originality, and it was this taste that was most positively displayed when the production of ceramics, carried along on the wave of developing commercialism, was at length transformed into mass production. In particular, the kilns of Mino and Seto, in the region from which Oribe originally came, entered a period of flourishing activity, moving in the vanguard of the new mercantile age. Because of its special emphasis on pattern, the Oribe taste was most effectively expressed in tableware, for here there was unlimited freedom to alter shapes and designs. Even today the Oribe-ware bowls, plates, *mukozuke* (side-dish containers; Fig. 87), and other dishes, with their distinctive green-and-white glazes, still fascinate people as examples of the highest achievement in this genre of ceramic art.

Here, by means of an excerpt from Sotan's diary, let us observe Oribe's tea style as it was revealed at a party given around the time when he first began to display his strikingly individual taste.

"Morning tea party at Fushimi, [lunar] February 28, 1599. Attended by the imperial adviser of Aki Province [Mori Terumoto], the chamberlain of Kurume [Kobayakawa Hidetsutsumi], and Sotan [Kamiya Sotan].

"Held in a 3-plus-a-*daime*-mat tearoom furnished with a double hanging shelf on whose upper level rested a charcoal scuttle. A thin board was attached to the lower end of the bamboo supporting the shelf. Over the sunken hearth was a new kettle of the *ubaguchi* [old woman's mouth] type, a kind with a raised rim, placed on a trivet.

"While the guests were washing their hands at the basin [*chozubachi*], the host removed the scroll from the tokonoma and placed a white camellia in the basket. A fresh-water jar of unglazed earthenware, its ladle hung on the wall. Alongside the jar, a high-shouldered tea caddy in a damask silk bag. The tea scoop, whisk, and napkin in the Koryo tea bowl. Blue celadon container for waste water. Lid

84. *Buddhist certificate written by I-shan I-ning (Issan Ichinei) and given to Kugan. Ink on paper; height, 27.6 cm.; length, 69 cm. 1314. Yamada family, Kyoto.*

85. *Water jar called Yaburebukuro (Torn Pouch). Iga ware; height, 21 cm. Late sixteenth century.*

86. *Tea bowl called Hagoromo (Robe of Feathers). Shino ware; diameter, 13.4 cm. Late sixteenth century.*

87. Side-dish containers (mukozuke) *designed by Furuta Oribe. Height of each container, 11 cm. Early seventeenth century.*

88. Section of Waka Makimono. *Poetry scroll with calligraphy by Hon'ami Koetsu over paintings* ▷
of cranes attributed to Tawaraya Sotatsu. Ink and colors on paper; dimensions of entire scroll:
height, 34.1 cm.; length, 1,460 cm. First half of seventeenth century.

rest of bamboo. A hanging scroll with calligraphy by I-shan I-ning, his signature on the lower right-hand side.

"The kettle was new, a large *ubaguchi* with a bronze lid. The latter had been found in Yoshino [in present Nara Prefecture]. The kettle matched it. The high-shouldered tea caddy was a Seto product. Yellow glaze and swollen base. Called a *tsujido* [wayside shrine]. It had a damask silk bag with violet cords. The height of the flower container-basket measured 1.2 to 1.3 *shaku* [about 36 to 39 centimeters]. On the shoulder was a handle. The base was diamond-shaped, while the mouth was round. The charcoal scuttle was shaped like a gourd. The tongs for the charcoal had handles of mulberry wood. The rings for lifting the kettle were of iron. An incense container of contemporary [Shino?] ware. A crane-feather brush to sweep the hearth.

"The water jar was Seto ware. The waste-water jar was a three-legged one of blue celadon. The tea bowls were large Koryo bowls, each with a slightly small mouth and a flaring base. They had scratch patterns on the surface. The crest was an arabesque, probably a peony. The tea bowls resembled celadon and had Mishima-style designs. For the thin tea, warped, funny-shaped Seto tea bowls were used."

From the large *ubaguchi* kettle, the I-shan I-ning calligraphy, the large Koryo tea bowls with the scratched design, the odd-shaped Seto tea bowls, and so on, we can see that works typical of Oribe's taste were already in use.

TEA BOWLS OF KOETSU Oribe's two successors guided his tea in different directions. On the one hand there emerged the world of the *daimyo cha* exemplified by Kobori Enshu (see Chapter Four), and on the other the *cha-no-yu* of the newly rising merchant class as symbolized in Hon'ami Koetsu.

That Koetsu was a disciple of both Oribe and Oda Uraku is well known from the *Nigiwai So,* a collection of essays on the *cha-no-yu,* Japanese poetry, and other topics written by Haiya Shoeki for his descendants and published in 1682. Yet his preference seems to have been for the tea style of Oribe, and it is probable that he was attracted to Oribe's originality in designing tea bowls. All the while, though, he strove to attain his own personal style, and the highly original works that emerged from his hands were to the last the achievement of a single man, in contrast with the Oribe-style tea ware, which depended on a group effort for its production. This individuality is what characterizes Koetsu's bowls, and it represents at the same time a new step toward the modernization of the arts of the *cha-no-yu.* Among the works of art left by Koetsu, the most remarkable are the Raku-ware tea bowls and his works of calligraphy.

The most brilliant calligraphy he produced is found in the *Waka Makimono* (Scrolls of Japanese Poetry), for which the poems were chosen from such well known anthologies as the *Sanjuroku-nin Shu* (Thirty-six Poets' Anthology) of the mid-Heian period and the *Shin Kokin-shu* (New Ancient and Modern Collection) of the early thirteenth century. On scrolls of writing paper, over background paintings attributed to Sotatsu, Koetsu inscribed the poems of the *Waka Makimono* in a style of calligraphy known as *sokuhitsu*—that is, by holding his brush at an angle rather than in the ordinary upright position. Each scroll has a different background design, and the themes include grasses and flowers of the four seasons (Fig. 65), deer, cranes (Fig. 88), and lotuses. These works were created in the early seventeenth century, when Koetsu was about fifty years old, and the style he displays in them is very much that of a man in the prime of life.

Most of his tea bowls, as far as we know today,

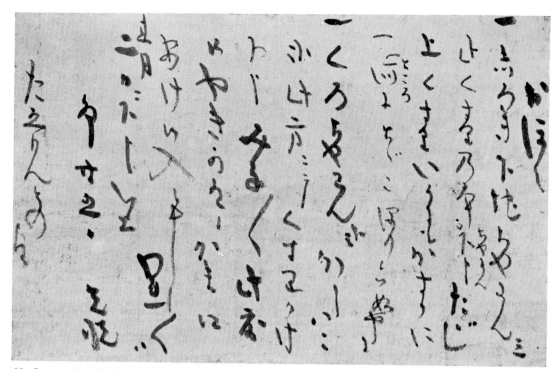

89. Letter written by Hon'ami Koetsu to Taemon. Ink on paper; height, 27.5 cm.; length 43.7 cm. Early seventeenth century. Sezu family, Tokyo.

were made in the space of ten years, beginning about 1620. To this period belong the late years of his life, after he had taken up residence at the so-called Koetsu Village in Takagamine. Among the bowls considered representative are the Seppo (Snow-covered Peak; Figs. 66, 195), the Otogoze (Homely Woman; Fig. 67), the Shigure (Autumn Rain; Fig. 68), the Fujisan (Mount Fuji; Figs. 12, 69), the Amagumo (Rain Clouds), the Shoji (Sliding Paper Door), and the Bishamon-do (Temple of Bishamon). Every one of these works is an expression of his absorbing passion for refined style, and in each of them can be felt the influence of a delicate creative impulse moving him to try his hand at new and varied forms of expression. As a result they permit a broad appreciation of his ingenuity.

Even though the tea bowls produced by both Koetsu and Chojiro were of Raku ware, the unique creative ingenuity revealed in the works of Koetsu is not to be found in those of Chojiro, from which all idiosyncrasy is shut out. In fact, Koetsu's works may be termed the first really personal achievement by a single artist in the field of Japanese pottery. Haiya Shoeki, in his *Nigiwai So*, refers to this accomplishment as "that which they speak of as interesting and possessed of character." What actually gave Koetsu's works their character was his search for nonorthodox forms not to be found in the works of artisan potters. He embodied at its fullest the free spirit of the Momoyama period as reflected in the words "any utensils may be used for the tea ceremony as long as their shape is good," and the tea utensils of the "informal" style inherited from Rikyu and Oribe achieved through him a "beauty of the unorthodox."

CHAPTER FOUR

—•—

Rusticity Refined

In the early seventeenth century the Tokugawa shogunate instituted a policy of national isolation, gradually sweeping out the influence of Christianity and bringing foreign trade under central control. In the 1630s overseas travel by Japanese subjects was banned, and heavier restrictions were imposed on foreign trade. This political shift coincided with a great change in the mood of society. It was a time when the system whereby the shogunate in Edo ruled over the fief-governing daimyo took firm hold and the feudalistic order grew stronger. As this sequence of events proceeded, the free creative spirit that had characterized the Momoyama age gradually waned. Hon'ami Koetsu died in the second lunar month of 1637, and his death was regarded as something like a symbol of this disappearing spirit.

ENSHU AND THE DAIMYO STYLE OF TEA With the advent of the Edo period (1603–1868), who would appear to provide leadership in the cult of tea and its idea of beauty? The man destined to fill the gap was a disciple of Oribe's who, following Oribe's death by seppuku, became tea instructor to the third Tokugawa shogun, Iemitsu (1604–51) —namely, Kobori Enshu Masakazu (1579–1647). In the service of Toyotomi Hideyoshi he became titular governor of Totomi Province (present Shizuoka Prefecture) and was therefore called Enshu, an alternate name for the province. After the Tokugawa shogunate began its rule, he succeeded his father as lord of Matsuyama in Iyo Province (present Ehime Prefecture), inheriting the annual stipend of 13,000 *koku* (about 65,000 bushels) of rice. Where he really displayed his skills, however, was in the work that occupied the greater part of his lifetime—that is to say, as commissioner for construction and also as magistrate of Kawachi (Osaka) and Omi provinces and of Fushimi in Kyoto. His imprint remained clearly visible on monumental architectural works by the samurai of early modern times, which included the donjon of Nagoya Castle (1612), the main compound and reception room of Fushimi Castle (1617), Nijo Castle (1603), the Sento Gosho (retired emperor's palace; 1624–29), the west compound of Edo Castle (1629), and Mito Castle (1629). His work as magistrate of Fushimi would alone suffice to show the range of his talents. Yet, what contributed most to his success as a construction administrator, more even than his being a samurai, was that he lived the true life of a *sukisha*.

Enshu's tea belongs in the line of the so-called *daimyo cha*. The examination of his outstanding works, however, raises doubts as to whether he ever fully grasped the meaning of *furyu*. This word, in its original meaning, denotes "the styles passed on from preceding generations, the manners bequeathed by outstanding men." It thus contains the concept of tradition and, if read with a slightly different pronunciation, also signifies creative in-

genuity. In the *Kobori Enshu Kakisute-bumi* (Private Scribblings of Kobori Enshu), writings in classical Japanese about the basic meaning of *cha-no-yu*, we find the following: "The mist in spring, a cuckoo half-hidden by greenish leaves in summer, a lonely-looking sunset in autumn, a snowy dawn in winter —in each of these, a feeling of the *cha-no-yu*." We see here a mode of expression similar to that used in such traditional Japanese literature as the *Makura no Soshi* (Pillow Book) by the mid-Heian court lady Sei Shonagon and the *Kokin-shu* (Ancient and Modern Collection), an anthology of Japanese poems selected by Ki no Tsurayuki (868?–945?). Enshu himself gave proof of a thorough classical education—for example, in the way he chose names from famous old verses for the *chuko meibutsu* tea caddies and tea ladles. (The *chuko*, or "rediscovered," *meibutsu*, it should be noted, are the tea utensils of good taste that Enshu himself selected and added to the existing *meibutsu*.) He adorned the tokonoma not only with calligraphic scrolls but

also with *utagire* (fragments of scrolls inscribed with traditional Japanese poetry), *waka kaishi* (poetry written on special writing paper), and *kasen-e* (portraits of famous poets inscribed with poetry). With these as a basis, moreover, he fashioned his new creations with an exceedingly delicate sensitivity. Nowhere did this sensitivity stand out more than in his care over the smallest details when designing teahouses and gardens, which won for his works the commendatory designation of *kirei sabi*, a term normally used to denote a highly sophisticated form of construction with its roots in the Heian period. Presupposed by *kirei sabi* is *sabi* itself—that is, elegant simplicity—which in turn presupposes *wabi*. *Wabi* is most frequently mentioned in connection with Rikyu's *soan cha-no-yu*, but here we would rather think of it as typical of Sotan. *Sabi* contained elements in common with *wabi*. Yet, with the passing of the Momoyama period and its revival of classicism, there emerged a concept of beauty where light was concealed in the depths of *wabi*. This

◁ 90. *Kobori Enshu's letter of condolence on the death of Hon'ami Koetsu. Ink on paper. 1637. Koetsu-ji, Kyoto.*

92. *Enshu-style water container and lid of its box, by Doshi. Seventeenth century. Kobori family, Tokyo.*

91. *Incense container in shape of mandarin duck, by Ninsei. Height, 4.9 cm. Seventeenth century. Yamato Bunkakan, Nara.*

hidden light was then drawn out by polishing, resulting in a refined *kirei sabi*.

Enshu, though his work was founded in classical beauty, nonetheless made a declaration of belief in feudal ethics, as shown in the opening sentence of his *Private Scribblings*: "The way of tea . . . contains nothing very new, consisting simply of loyalty and filial piety, the diligent execution of the business of each household, and above all the need to insure that old friendships do not die." Here, at the same time, we have just what constituted the basis of the *daimyo cha*, whence it may be said that in Enshu artistic creation flourished side by side with political opportunism.

SOWA AND THE COURT STYLE OF TEA

Kobori Enshu's appearance in samurai society coincided with the emergence of another figure in the society of the court nobles. His name was Kanamori Shigechika (1584–1656). The turning point in his life

was the Winter Siege of Osaka Castle. His family had been followers of Hideyoshi, but after Hideyoshi's death and his vassals' defeat in the Battle of Sekigahara they joined forces with Tokugawa Ieyasu. Shigechika is thought to have retained his affection for Hideyoshi, and when he was called to fight under Ieyasu in the Winter Siege, he refused to go. Disowned by his father, he discarded his samurai rank and became a lay priest, changing his name to Sowa. In Kyoto he made the acquaintance of such notables as Konoe Ozan (1599–1649), an outstanding tea man, and Ichijo Ekan, both sons of Emperor Goyozei (1571–1617; r. 1586–1611). He also taught the *cha-no-yu* to Tofukumon-in (1607–78), the consort of Emperor Gomizuno-o, and had close connections with the court. His tea showed a remarkable delicacy, the fruit of its association with *kirei sabi*. Mention is also made of him in the *Kaiki*, by Yamashina Doan, a book about the life and doings of Konoe Iehiro (1667–1736), a leading noble of the time. It relates how

93. *Tea bowl and lid of its box, which bears the Kanamori Sowa inscription "Old Karatsu with curvilinear design." Decorated Karatsu (E-garatsu) ware; diameter, 12.5 cm. Early seventeenth century. Idemitsu family, Tokyo.*

one day Prince Ekan invited Sowa and requested that he serve tea using the *daisu*. Sowa positioned himself in front of the *daisu* and took the ladle in his hands, then went into the anteroom and broke a piece off its handle, shortening it by 5 *bu*, or about 1.5 centimeters. This action completely won for him the trust of Prince Ekan. It was the delicate and sophisticated touch he showed in events such as this that won for him the title Hime (princess), a term usually reserved for young ladies of birth, which suggests his extreme refinement. Yet what ultimately made him famous was his discovery of the renowned ceramist from Omuro in Kyoto, Nonomura Ninsei (1598–1666), to whose wares Sowa gave the name Omuro pottery, today used to denote the pottery of the area around the Ninna-ji temple in that same city. Sowa guided Ninsei in the making of his works and acted as a dealer with would-be purchasers. He also designed utensil boxes with round-edged lids (Fig. 93). These were

known as "Sowa boxes," and he inscribed them in his own hand. It is also said that among Ninsei's works were some on which he wrote Ninsei's signature for the latter to carve, thus giving rise to the term "Sowa seals." This close relationship between the two men, reaching as deep as the very content of their artistic creation, enabled Sowa to communicate to Ninsei his own aesthetic sense, and the elegant and gentle feeling pervading Ninsei's art can be said to have constituted the very essence of the imperial-court tea and of Sowa's ideals.

Sowa was that kind of man. With Kyoto as the center of his activities he exerted widespread influence, and the expression "Kanamori's authoritative message" was a catch phrase among lovers of tea that even the celebrated novelist Ihara Saikaku (1642–93) used in his *Nippon Eitaigura* (The Japanese Family Storehouse), one of the *ukiyo zoshi*, a new genre of realistic literature he helped to introduce. Kamigata, or the area centering in Kyoto,

94. Tea caddy called Osaka Marutsubo. Old Seto ware; height, 8.5 cm. Sixteenth or seventeenth century. Nezu Art Museum, Tokyo.

95. Korean tea bowl called Nagasaki Katade. Diameter, 14.6 cm. Yi dynasty, fifteenth or sixteenth century. Nezu Art Museum, Tokyo.

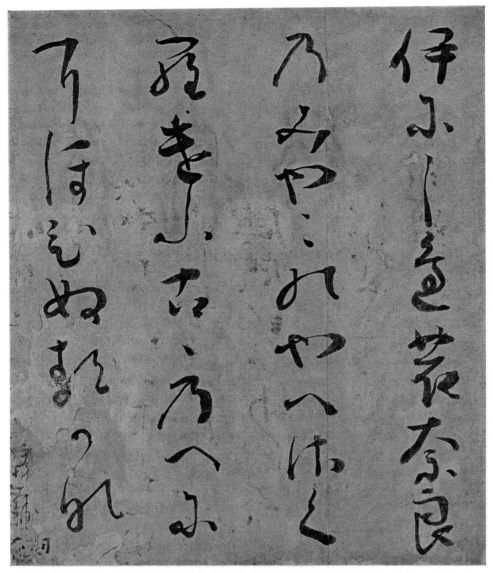

98. Ogura Shikishi *calligraphy, attributed to Fujiwara Teika. Ink and colors on paper; height, 18.7 cm.; width, 16.6 cm. Thirteenth century. Kani family, Aichi Prefecture.*

99. *Interior view of Jiko-in tearoom, showing tokonoma at rear.* ▷
Designed by Katagiri Sekishu. 1671. Nara Prefecture.

100. Tearoom of Ichijo E-kan's Nishikamo Villa. About 1646. Yamada family, Kanagawa Prefecture.

101. *Incense burner in shape of pheasant, by Nonomura Ninsei. Height, 18 cm. Seventeenth century. Ishikawa Prefectural Art Museum, Kanazawa, Ishikawa Prefecture.*

*102. Shelves and cabinet in anteroom to tearoom of Ichijo Ekan's Nishikamo Villa.
About 1646. Yamada family, Kanagawa Prefecture. (See also Figures 109, 200.)*

◁ *103 (opposite page). Interior view of Kasumi-doko no Seki shoin room, designed by Konoike Ryoei. 1742. Gyoku-rin-in, Daitoku-ji, Kyoto.*

104 (above). Azaleas and Running Water, *by Ogata Korin. Colors on cloth; height, 39.6 cm.; width, 60.5 cm. Seventeenth century. Hatakeyama Museum, Tokyo.*

105. Incense container with design of plum blossoms, by Ogata Kenzan. Height, 4.8 cm. Seventcenth century. Fujita Art Museum, Osaka.

106. Kinrande (gold-decorated) water vessel with design of flowers and birds. Height, 21.2 cm. Ming dynasty, sixteenth century. Goto Art Museum, Tokyo.

107. *Interior view of Inari Shrine teahouse. First half of seventeenth century. Fushimi Inari Shrine, Kyoto.*

where Sowa's tea was notably successful, also witnessed the birth of Katagiri Sekishu (1605–73), who followed Enshu as the third tea instructor to the Tokugawa household and may well have been among those who came knocking at Sowa's door. He was characterized, accordingly, by a broad-minded attitude that absorbed the attitudes of both the imperial court and the shogunate.

SEKISHU AND THE PERFECTED DAIMYO TEA

Katagiri Sekishu advanced *daimyo cha* beyond the stage attained by Enshu and was responsible as well for synthesizing this style of tea with that of the court and bringing it to perfection. He was the second son of Katagiri Sadataka, younger brother of Katagiri Katsumoto (1556–1615), a retainer of Toyotomi Hideyoshi, and was given the name Sadamasa. He took lessons in tea from Kuwayama Sosen (1560–1632), a disciple of Rikyu's eldest son, Doan. On his mother's side he was the great-grandson of Rikyu's friend Imai Sokyu, thus living from the start in a natural tea atmosphere. In 1624 he became titular governor of Iwami Province (present Shimane Prefecture) and received a fief from his father, thus also becoming a daimyo with an annual stipend of 10,000 *koku* (about 50,000 bushels) of rice at Koizumi in Yamato Province (present Nara Prefecture). It was then that his tea name came to the fore. In Kyoto he practiced Zen under Gyokushitsu Sohaku (1572–1641), abbot of the Daitoku-ji temple, and received the Buddhist name of Sanshuku Sokan. In time he built the Korin-an teahouse beside the Hoshun-in, the sub-temple erected by his teacher, Gyokushitsu, in the Daitoku-ji compound.

108. *Naka-no-bo Shoin of Taima-dera, Nara Prefecture.*

His ideas were handed down to posterity in the *Wabi no Fumi* (Letter Concerning Wabi Tea), which he wrote in 1661, stressing the significance of *wabi* in the *cha-no-yu*. This document shows him to have been Jo-o's follower in matters of style, to the extent that he even went as far as to relocate Jo-o's tearoom at the Korin-an. Thus he moved counter to the daimyo of his time, who, regardless of their social rank, were groping in vain for the sentiment of *sabi*. He advocated instead the *hiroma* (large reception room) style of tea suited to the concept of *daimyo cha*, at the same time pursuing his study of the traditional spirit of the *cha-no-yu*, by which means he was able to give clear expression to the foundation of his ideal. That is, in view of Sekishu's reactionary tendency, the tea best suited to him was not Rikyu's *soan cha-no-yu* but, without going back as far as Juko, that of Jo-o. Saying this does not, of course, alter the fact that Sekishu's style was the one that best conformed to the realities of the tea

world in his day. Although his way of tea displayed neither the religious severity of Rikyu nor the cultural intelligence of Enshu, it was characterized by a breadth of spirit that embraced both of these and by a slight trace of Juko's aristocratic taste, all of which made it no effort for him to charm the people of his time. Here was laid the foundation for a theory of the *cha-no-yu* as an entertainment not only for the daimyo but also for the merchant class.

In 1663 Sekishu built the Jiko-in teahouse on his estate at Koizumi in Yamato and likewise erected a tearoom to his taste on the grounds of the Naka-no-bo priest's residence at the Taima-dera temple, also in Yamato. Soon after this he was appointed tea instructor to the fourth Tokugawa shogun, Ietsuna (1641–80). Then in 1666 he proceeded to Kyoto at the request of the retired emperor Gosai (1637–85; r. 1656–63) to design the garden of the latter's residence, the Sento Gosho, and at this same time we find him initiating the imperial prince

109. *Interior view of Ichijo Ekan's Nishikamo Villa teahouse. About 1646; relocated in 1959. Yamada family, Kanagawa Prefecture.*

Gyonen, who was a priest at the Myoho-in temple in Kyoto, into the way of the 1.5-mat-room *cha-no-yu.* There are two probable explanations for this event: first, his good connection with Tofuku-mon-in, whence may have come his acquaintance with Sowa, and second, an explanation that springs more readily to mind, the fact that the Taima-dera was honored by a visit from the retired emperor. In preparation for this visit, Sekishu built the *shoin* of the Naka-no-bo (Fig. 108) and an attached tearoom. The fact that both are built in his style would seem to indicate that the Naka-no-bo provided the occasion for a bond between the shogun's instructor Sekishu and the ex-emperor. Subsequent to this, Sekishu assumed in the tea world a role similar to that performed by Tofukumon-in in the wide cultural sphere of the court.

It was in 1668 that Sekishu resigned his position with the shogunate. After his resignation, the post of instructor to the shogun's household was abol-ished in every field of art because of the necessity for the shogun to manifest supreme authority. The same time saw an overwhelming expansion of Sekishu's authority, and he came entirely to dominate the world of tea as the *iemoto* (hereditary grand master) in the old sense—that is, he personally taught each and every one of his disciples and bestowed on them certificates of proficiency that authorized them to teach and, in turn, to bestow certificates on others. (In the present system only the *iemoto* himself is authorized to bestow certificates.)

THE SERVER'S SEAT AS THE STAGE FOR A PERFORMANCE Rikyu's successors all favored using the *daime-gamae,* a tearoom structure with a *daime* mat and the so-called central post. This style was known as the "core of the *soan*" because it represented the essence of the *soan* style. As the minimum structure

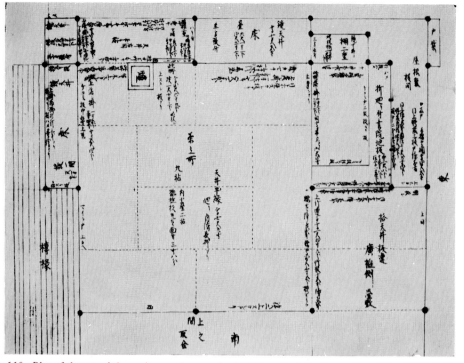

110. *Plan of* chatate-dokoro *(tea-serving room) of Takinomoto-bo teahouse. From* Juhachi Kakoi no Zu *(Drawings of Eighteen Teahouses). National Diet Library, Tokyo. (See also Foldout 2.)*

required for a tearoom, it could be very practically adapted to any space.

Rikyu's basic principle had been to use the mat directly in front of the tokonoma as the seat of honor and to place the mat for the host—that is the *temaeza,* or server's seat—toward the subordinate positions. Uraku, Oribe, and Enshu, on the other hand, attempted a freer location of the server's seat, usually selecting a position close to the tokonoma. At an earlier time, Uraku had already even tried placing the host beside the tokonoma— the so-called host's-tokonoma (*teishu-doko*) style—in the 3-plus-a-*daime*-mat room at the Kyusho-in temple in Temma (Osaka), and Oribe almost invariably built his tearooms with the tokonoma toward the subordinate positions, as in the En-an teahouse. In this trend we can see a shift from the spiritual attitude of regarding the server's seat as a place lower in rank than the guests' seats to that of seeing

in it a stagelike device aimed at putting on a show for the guests. Here the paper windows (*shikishi mado*), devised by Oribe, became a most effective piece of stage equipment for the server's seat.

This transformation of the server's seat into a stage had already been partially completed in the En-an. As the tendency progressed even further, the server's seat was set on a level with the guest mats by being placed in their midst, a device frequently found in Enshu's tearooms. The tearoom he installed in his Fushimi mansion followed this pattern. Another device commonly used was to place the tokonoma and the server's seat end to end as illustrated in the Hasso no Seki at the Konchi-in (Fig. 111), a subtemple of the Nanzen-ji in Kyoto, and likewise in the Bosen tearoom in the Koho-an (Figs. 71, 116) of the Daitoku-ji. There was also a style, condemned by Oribe but attempted frequently by Enshu, with an open-

111. *Interior view of Hasso no Seki tearoom, designed by Kobori Enshu. About 1628. Konchi-in, Nanzen-ji, Kyoto.*

timbered ceiling (ceiling with rafters exposed to the interior) above the server's seat and a skylight opened in the roof, the purpose being to achieve an effect similar to that of floodlighting on a stage. This process of transforming the server's seat into a stage reached its climax with Enshu. Here, too, in this drive toward converting the *cha-no-yu* into a show that would include both the display of utensils and the performance on stage, so to speak, we can discern the aim that was the ideal of daimyo tea.

TEAROOMS IN THE ENSHU STYLE

After resigning from his post as tea instructor to the shogun, Enshu returned to Kyoto, where he lived in comfortable retirement at his Roku Jizo mansion in Fushimi. Much of his time was taken up with tea parties attended by numerous celebrities, among them

Sekishu and Yoken. To this residence belonged, besides the 4.5-plus-a-*daime*-mat tearoom (*sukiya*) called the Shosui-tei, teahouses such as the Tengo-an and Joshu-an. Theirs was the style most typical of Enshu—a style that he also employed in the Takinomoto-bo at the Iwashimizu Hachiman-gu shrine (Fig. 110) to the south of Kyoto and in other places. A *dobisashi* (earth-floored lean-to) flanked the south side of the Shosui-tei, with a *nijiri-guchi* in the middle. By this means two lines of movement, left and right, were fashioned within the room, one leading toward the tokonoma and the space reserved for use by the highest-ranking guest and the other toward the other participants' seats. The originality of Enshu's technique lay in not devising separate seats for the accompanying participants, as Oribe had done, but rather distinguishing the upper and lower ranks clearly by their location vis-à-vis the entrance. Another feature of

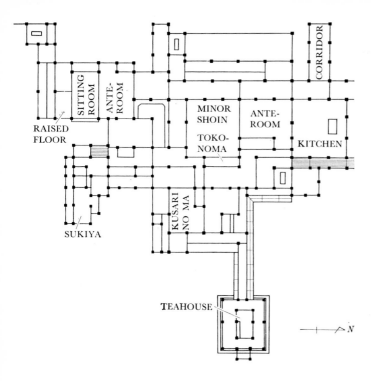

SITTING ROOM

ANTE-ROOM

CORRIDOR

RAISED FLOOR

MINOR SHOIN

ANTE-ROOM

TOKO-NOMA

KITCHEN

KUSARI NO MA

SUKIYA

TEAHOUSE

N

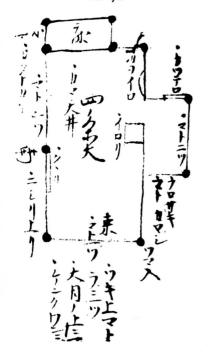

Sukiya

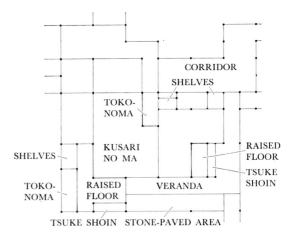

Kusari no Ma

CORRIDOR

SHELVES

TOKO-NOMA

SHELVES

KUSARI NO MA

RAISED FLOOR

TSUKE SHOIN

TOKO-NOMA

RAISED FLOOR

VERANDA

TSUKE SHOIN

STONE-PAVED AREA

112. *Top: redrawn plan of Kobori Enshu's Fushimi mansion, from* Joshu Fushimi Gokyutaku no Zu *(Plan of the Former Mansion in Fushimi). Saji family, Shiga Prefecture. Left: plan of* sukiya *in Enshu's Fushimi mansion, from* Matsuya Kaiki *(Tea Records of Matsuya). Above: redrawn plan of* kusari no ma *in Enshu's Fushimi mansion, from an old drawing owned by the Nakai family.*

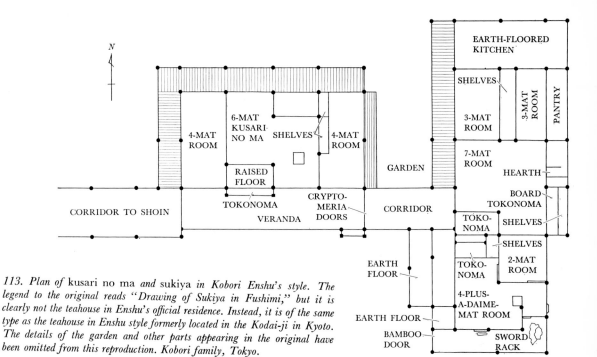

113. *Plan of* kusari no ma *and* sukiya *in Kobori Enshu's style. The legend to the original reads "Drawing of Sukiya in Fushimi," but it is clearly not the teahouse in Enshu's official residence. Instead, it is of the same type as the teahouse in Enshu style formerly located in the Kodai-ji in Kyoto. The details of the garden and other parts appearing in the original have been omitted from this reproduction. Kobori family, Tokyo.*

the room was that it had twelve windows, the three skylights included. In this respect Enshu inherited Oribe's liking for numerous windows, but he gave them a much more lively distribution than his predecessor had done. According to the *Matsuya Kaiki* (Tea Records of Matsuya), the room had a thatched roof, and the tokonoma was finished with a rough coat of plaster, which probably gave it an appearance resembling that of the *soan*-style room.

This tearoom was connected to the *kusari no ma* by a corridor running north from its host's entrance. From a point north of the *kusari no ma*, in turn, a roofed passage extended eastward and connected with the teahouse. On the west side of the *kusari no ma* there was a small *shoin* together with living quarters (Fig. 112). In his *Matsuya Nikki* (Diary of Matsuya) the merchant Matsuya Hisashige writes: "It is possible to go from the host's entrance to the *kusari no ma* and from there to the *shoin* and the teahouse. The layout on the way is of a routine style, such as not to draw too much attention, so that it becomes difficult to recollect and write down exactly what forms of decoration there are." Thus it was possible to go from one room to another by means of the corridors, and both the tearoom and the teahouse became joined as in one building to the *kusari no ma* and the *shoin*, which were appropriately decorated. Therein lay the distinctive feature of Enshu's *sukiya* (teahouse) layout, of which Figure 113 offers a good example.

Enshu's *kusari no ma* in his Fushimi mansion revealed a far greater complexity when compared with Oribe's and was provided with embellishments in no way inferior to those of the *shoin*. This *kusari no ma* consisted of two rooms. The main one lay to the south and featured a raised-floor area (*jodan*) in the southeast corner, complete with a tokonoma, staggered shelves, and a *tsuke shoin*. In the lower part of the same room, to the north, was a 6-*shaku* tokonoma. In the anteroom, on the north, a raised-

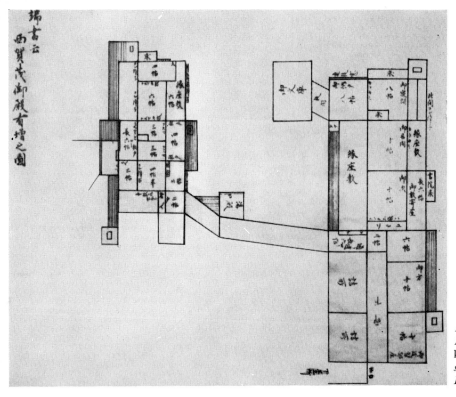

114. *Plan of Ichijo Ekan's Nishikamo Villa, from* On-ko Roku. *The teahouse shown at left is still extant. Daigo family, Tokyo.*

floor area was installed to the north, furnished with a *tsuke shoin*. Next to the raised-floor area was the server's seat. On the west side of the anteroom and slightly to the north were placed staggered shelves.

In 1636, at the request of Tokugawa Iemitsu, Enshu acted as host at a tea party in Shinagawa in Edo. On his return to Fushimi a year later he built the Tengo-an, a teahouse furnished with a *tsuke shoin* and a board-floor tokonoma forming a right angle on the raised portion of the floor.

In the Takinomoto-bo, the residence of one of Enshu's famous disciples, Shokado Shojo (1584–1639), there was a tearoom called the Kan'un-ken, as well as other rooms in the style of Enshu. These rooms featured a truly remarkable construction of the shelves, and it must have been an eye-opening experience to witness the employment of every conceivable form of ornamentation and the skillful

introduction of changes and fresh ideas in structure and design. Enshu carried the "core of the *soan*"—namely, the *daime-gamae*—into the very sitting room, thereby uniting tea with the decoration of the room itself. His style of tea was despised by the followers of Rikyu's school, who ridiculed it with such denunciations as "Collecting old utensils, he loads the shelves with them" and "It looks as though he had set up a shop for selling Chinese goods." These comments are recorded in the *Chajin Keifu* (Genealogy of Tea Men), compiled by Suzuki Masamichi in 1796.

Nevertheless, Enshu's decoration of the tearoom was not a revival of the custom of the Higashiyama period. Instead, it followed the line of thought that "it is fundamental to ornament with few things, and these must not stand out." He frequently made use of a variety of openwork designs in the transom, in

115. *Interior views of Mittan tearoom, designed by Kobori Enshu, showing display shelves on left. About 1638. Ryoko-in, Daitoku-ji, Kyoto.*

the wainscoting of the *sode kabe* (extended wall attached to the central post by the tokonoma), and around the shelves. (See Foldout 2.) One can still see an example of such openwork in the ornamental shelves of the Mittan tearoom in the Ryoko-in subtemple of the Daitoku-ji (Fig. 115). By arranging the utensils in a setting of artistic design, Enshu strove to give a moderate tone to the display itself.

The Mittan tearoom (Figs. 11, 115) is usually said to be in Enshu's style, but the date when it was built is not clear. According to drawings made by Matsuya Hisashige at the tea party given in 1641 by the abbot Kogetsu, Enshu's teacher in the practice of Zen, it originally stood apart from the *shoin*, with a veranda on two sides and the entrance on the side that now adjoins the *shoin*. The stepping-stone approach to the veranda had small stones strewn around it, there was shrubbery nearby, and

the ground was covered with pine needles. Usage at the time differed from that of the present day in the respect that at Kogetsu's tea party a work of calligraphy by the Zen abbot Mittan (from whom the tearoom takes its name) was hung in a genuine tokonoma rather than in the place now known as the "Mittan tokonoma." In Kogetsu's time the Mittan tokonoma, where Mittan's calligraphy is hung today, was called a *tsuke shoin* and represented the *shoin* style of construction.

Besides the tokonoma, the shelves, and the *tsuke shoin*, this 4.5-plus-a-*daime*-mat tearoom incorporated high-dadoed *shoji* (sliding doors of translucent paper pasted over wooden latticework frames) and *nageshi* (ornamental beamlike bands running above the posts) inserted into the papered walls. In other words, it formed a combination of the *shoin* and the *soan*. Yet the two styles did not clash. In the *daime-*

116. *Interior view of Bosen tearoom, designed by Kobori Enshu. Originally built about 1644; rebuilt in 1797. Koho-an, Daitoku-ji, Kyoto.*

gamae the extended wall was fitted with a board of cryptomeria wood showing a central design in the grain. This freed the room from the typical flavor of the *soan* and gave it the neat, orderly style characteristic of the *shoin*. Enshu used a tokonoma post made of a log with the bark intact. The other posts were square-cut timbers with the bark left on the four corners. He likewise communicated the feeling of tea to the structure of the shelves and to the design of the openwork. What he was really attempting was a blend of the two styles, and with *kirei sabi* as the keynote he succeeded skillfully in investing the room with a sense of unity.

In this way, Enshu pursued the ideal of the tea of samurai society, which was to express, by means of the *shoin*, a standard that had always been identified with the *soan*. The consummation of this ideal was embodied at the Bosen tearoom (Figs. 71, 116) of the Koho-an in the Daitoku-ji.

The Bosen has the architectural appearance of the stylish *shoin*, furnished with *nageshi* running between square pillars, papered walls, and two verandas—a high, broad one with a balustrade at one end and a low one of less than usual height. The tearoom makes no use of the *daime-gamae* or of any other elements typical of the *soan*, but, starting with the juxtaposition of the tokonoma and the server's seat, the style is peculiarly Enshu's, and the structure of the room is well rounded off. Moreover, the *nageshi* encircles the entire room, thereby harmonizing the composure and dignity of the framework with the delicate *sunazuri* (sand-rubbed) texture of the cryptomeria ceiling and doing away with the stern appearance typical of the *shoin*. (The *sunazuri* effect was obtained by first rubbing the ceiling with sand and then rubbing it with whitewash.) Again, the peculiar design of the veranda edge draws the scenery of the inner garden into the room, thereby fostering a tea atmosphere. In fact, it was in the garden and the veranda that the designer of this

117. *View of approach to Shokin-tei teahouse, showing pond and stone bridge. Katsura Detached Palace, Kyoto.*

room displayed his greatest originality. The garden path begins at the lower end of the wide veranda adjoining the abbot's quarters, whence stepping-stones are laid in a line under the eaves. Advancing along them, one reaches the "shoe-leaving stone" (*kutsu-nugi ishi*) that serves as a step up in front of the lower veranda, and from there one enters the room. At this stage, what seems from inside the room to be simply an interesting arrangement of *shoji* above the veranda assumes the role of a *nijiri-guchi*. The stone hand-washing basin (*chozubachi*) at the edge of the veranda is set low so as to impede its use from a standing position, giving it the name *tsukubai*, or "crouching basin." Thus, even in the *shoin*-style construction, completely dissociated from that of the *soan*, could be found an arrangement shared by the *soan*—namely, the movement from the steppingstones past the stone basin to the *nijiri-guchi*.

Enshu himself confessed that "we tea men, in-

cluding Furuta Oribe, borrowed the outline of the teahouse style with a garden perfected by Rikyu." Ultimately, the transformation of the tearoom into a *shoin*, as illustrated in the case of the Bosen, could not avoid subordination to the "principle of the garden and *soan*." It was Enshu who attempted the style of tea most distant from Rikyu's, yet it was also he who grasped, perhaps better than any other, Rikyu's style of tea.

TEAHOUSES OF THE NOBILITY The main residence of the imperial prince Toshihito (1579–1629), forefather of the Katsura family and first owner of the celebrated villa now known as the Katsura Detached Palace, contained, in 1602, a *shoin*, a *sukiya*, and a *soan*, to which were added, in 1619, a 2-plus-a-*daime*-mat room and a *kusari no ma*. Facilities of this kind for tea parties were also common to buildings designed by Oribe and others. Oribe stated that "the tea-

118. *Tea bowl with design of folding fans and running water, by Nonomura Ninsei. Diameter, 13 cm. Second half of seventeenth century.*

119. *Entrance (left) and interior (right) of Teigyoku-ken teahouse, in Kanamori Sowa's style. About mid-seventeenth century. Shinju-an, Daitoku-ji, Kyoto.* ▷

house should have a thatched roof," and noblemen, too, fancied the form of the *soan* and made use of it. But they examined and criticized the styles of the influential tea masters and attempted to adhere to their own tastes without failing to display their own superior authority. In consequence, their *soan* could not help being affected by their traditional life style and their aesthetic sense, which was highly respectful of conventional practices. Teahouses that reveal clearly the qualities characteristic of the *soan* fashioned to the taste of the nobles are those at the Katsura Detached Palace, the one formerly at Ichijo Ekan's Nishikamo Villa in Kyoto and now in Kanagawa Prefecture, and the Toshin-tei teahouse, said to have been in the style favored by the retired emperor Gomizuno-o. The outstanding characteristic of these structures can be seen in the matted veranda around the tearoom and, in the case of Ekan's villa, a 6-*shaku*-wide mat-floored

veranda on two sides of the sitting room. This feature gave the building a noble air and wider floor space despite its having the exterior appearance of a rustic cottage. Nor could the nobles, being fond of ornamentation, resist placing display shelves even in a 3-plus-a-*daime*-mat teahouse like the Toshin-tei. The proliferation of materials used in the construction of the *soan* aroused their appetite for design, and the result was a graceful and lighthearted style apparent even in the wainscoting and the finger grips of the sliding partitions.

In the teahouse of Ekan's villa (Figs. 100, 109) the three-mat anteroom in the "lower position" is provided with a two-level shelf (Fig. 102), the work of Kanamori Sowa, according to the *Onko Roku* (Review of the Past), a record of the Daigo family. The plans for the entire teahouse were probably submitted to Sowa for his opinion. He was the inheritor of Oribe's style of design, which he formal-

ized even further. Another teahouse said to be in his style is the Teigyoku-ken in the Shinju-an at the Daitoku-ji (Fig. 119). Although it has a mere 2-plus-a-*daime*-mat room, it has a court inside of the *nijiri-guchi*, which gives the whole house an ample feeling of spaciousness. Sowa did not see in the Tai-an simply a 2-mat room. He thought it fitting to perform the tea ceremony in a frame of mind that viewed the tearoom and the anteroom as one continuous space. In his opinion "the room should not appear cramped," and for this reason he always laid stress on devices that created ample space. This tendency to respect comfort explains in great measure why the works of Sowa met with such support from the nobles.

In 1663, Sekishu selected a picturesque site to the northeast of his mansion at Koizumi in Yamato Province and there erected the Jiko-in temple to perform religious rites in memory of his deceased parents. To the present day there remain at this temple a *shoin*, a tearoom, and a garden that reflect his taste. The *shoin*, provided with a tokonoma and a *tsuke shoin*, has as its basis the style of a commoner's house (*minka*) and is plain to the extent that it even does away with the *nageshi* ornamental bands. A wide wooden-floored veranda encircles the room, and from the garden hedge, trimmed low and round, can be enjoyed at leisure the view that extends as far as the distant Nara Hills. The tearoom (Fig. 99), on the northeast corner, is of the 2-plus-a-*daime*-mat size, a small *wabi*-style room. Directly across from the *nijiri-guchi* is the *daime* mat (server's seat). The tokonoma lies beyond the server's seat and is of the *teishu-doko* type. Between the guest seats and the *shoin* is a 2-mat anteroom. The ceiling shows a flat surface lined with thin cryptomeria boards, specially ordered from Nonè, Kochi Prefecture, and there rises to it a strikingly curved

120. Inscription reading "Bosen," by Kobori Enshu. Ink on paper; mounted on a plaque. First half of seventeenth century. Koho-an, Daitoku-ji, Kyoto.

121. Bamboo in Ink, by Takimoto Shokado, with inscription by Kobori Enshu. Ink on paper. First half of seventeenth century.

oaken central post with the bark intact. The room acquires a sense of expansion from the mullioned windows that fully span two sides of the guest seat in a right angle. Plain material is used throughout, effecting a light and fluent structure that reflects the designer's outstanding creative capacity. Seki-shu built his tea world, not with Rikyu's devotion to the pursuit of the ultimate, but based instead on a synthesis of *wabi* that included even the samurai style and the carefree, bright, and graceful style of the court nobles. It was an attitude that sought the comforts of life.

ENSHU'S STYLE OF TEA

The *wabi* tea that developed with Rikyu and Oribe was based on a merchant-class style of tea. But by the time of Enshu, who succeeded Oribe as the shogun's tea master, a different kind of tea ceremony had made its appearance—one that appealed to the daimyo class. In this new style of tea, however, there was none of the formal severity of the earlier *shoin* tea. What was sought instead was the staging of a tea performance that would suit the current tastes of the daimyo.

There is no doubt that Enshu's tea possessed neither the spiritual strength of Rikyu's nor the intense creative quality of Oribe's. It was, rather, a style of tea broad enough to admit many standards, richly varied according to the requirements of time and place and constantly striving to make the most of all the tea utensils of both old and contemporary times. Enshu felt it just as comfortable to perform in the 2-mat *soan* room as in the 4.5-mat room or in the large entertainment hall, and his technique was even capable of transforming the rigid *shoin*-style teahouse into an enjoyable place. Likewise rich in variety was his use of tea utensils, including Chinese, Korean, and Japanese wares, regardless of whether they were old or new. In this sense, no other tea man surpassed him in his interest in so many cultural objects. His style, commonly known as *kirei sabi*, or refined rusticity, could, to use another expression, also be termed romantic, and it was Enshu who first added a

Foldout 1: Evolution of the 4.5-Mat Tearoom in Sen no Rikyu's Style

RIKYU'S 4.5-MAT TEAROOM AS REVIVED BY SOTAN. The Yu-in, by Sen Sotan, had the characteristic appearance of the Rikyu-style 4.5-mat room, popularly favored in the Edo period. The corner post of the server's seat was the partly plastered "toothpick post"; the utensil-closet post had been eliminated; and a post was added in the wall containing the *nijiri-guchi*. The plastered part of the corner post was 3.3 *shaku* (about 1 meter) high. This was later increased, diminishing the visible portion of the post. The restoration drawings are based on plans made by Hisada Sozen (1646–1717), fourth-generation master of the Hisada school.

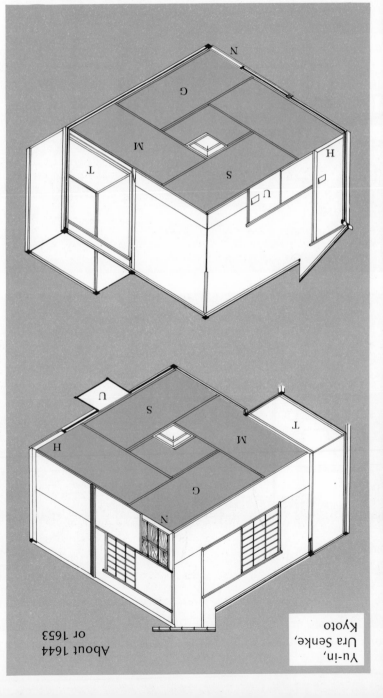

KEY

G = guests' seats
H = host's entrance
M = main guest's seat
N = *nijiri-guchi*
S = server's seat
T = tokonoma
U = utensil closet

About 1644
or 1653

Yu-in,
Ura Senke,
Kyoto

Takinomoto-bo Chatate-dokoro and Shoin, Iwashimizu Shrine, Kyoto

Soho's *Tearoom in Fushimi*, in the possession of Horiguchi Sutemi.

er's seat. The restoration drawings are based chiefly on the *Plans of Lord* three places: the earth-floored area (not shown), guests' seats, and serv-framed lattice window one above the other. Skylights were opened over and the method of placing the *nijiri-guchi*, mullioned windows, and un-*guchi*. Features also uniquely Enshu's were the large number of windows features of this room was the location of the server's seat and the *nijiri-*

similarly styled rooms in other places as well. One of the outstanding This is the most representative of the tearooms in Enshu's style; he built

4-plus-a-*daime*-mat type

Tearoom in Enshu's Fushimi Mansion, Kyoto

View of
Tokonoma
and Server's Seat

View from Server's
Entrance

o-an, Daitoku-ji, Kyoto

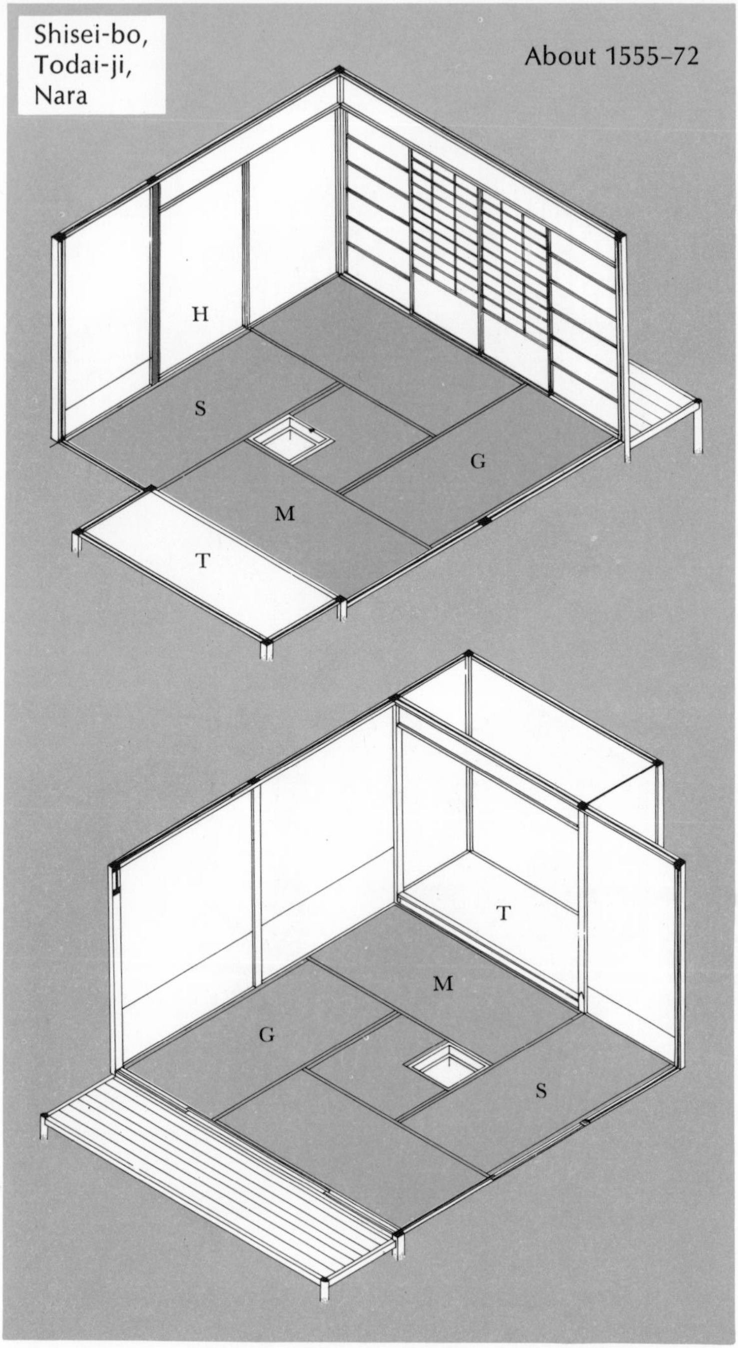

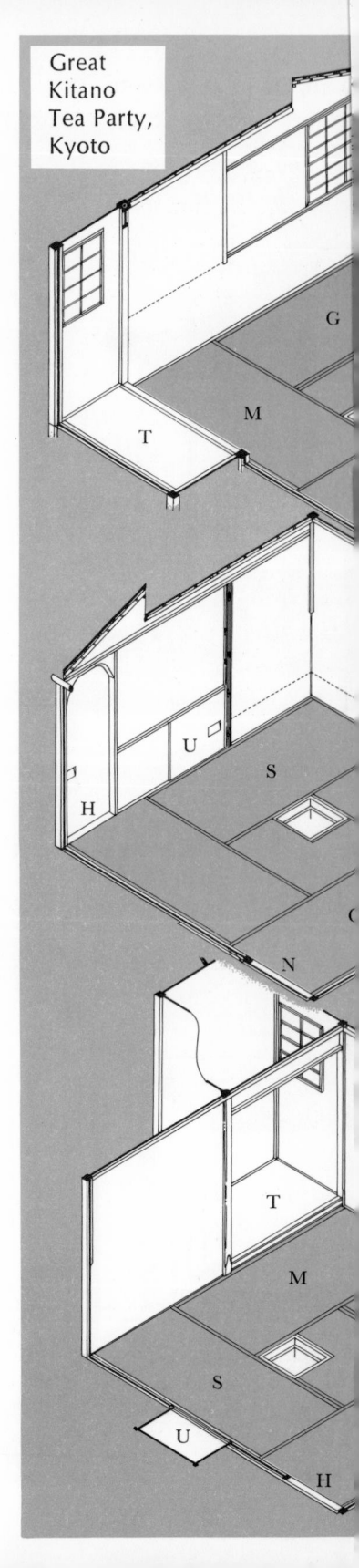

About 1555–72

Great Kitano Tea Party, Kyoto

THE 4.5-MAT TEAROOM IN THE SHISEI-BO, TODAI-JI, NARA. This room was in the style of Takeno Jo-o's 4.5-mat room, furnished with a veranda and a 6-*shaku* tokonoma. The mats were arranged in the reverse style. The restoration drawings are based chiefly on the stand-up paper models from the collection of Matsudaira Rakuo.

THE 4.5-MAT TEAROOM BUILT FOR THE GREAT KITANO TEA PARTY, KYOTO. This room ▷ featured a high tokonoma ceiling; a calligraphy window; posts by the *nijiriguchi* and the utensil closet; a corner post of the server's seat, coated with plaster part of the way up; and an extension of the host's-entrance lintel. A different restoration is conceivable for the host's entrance and the utensil closet. The restoration drawings are based chiefly on Hosokawa's book on the tea ceremony.

THE 4.5-MAT TEAROOM IN RIKYU'S JURAKU RESIDENCE, KYOTO. Here the post by the *nijiri-guchi* and the extended lintel had been dispensed with, leaving only the utensil-closet post intact. The location of the window in the side wall by the guests' seats had changed considerably from the preceding type. The restoration drawings are based on the carpenter's manual *Plans of Rikyu's Juraku Residence.*

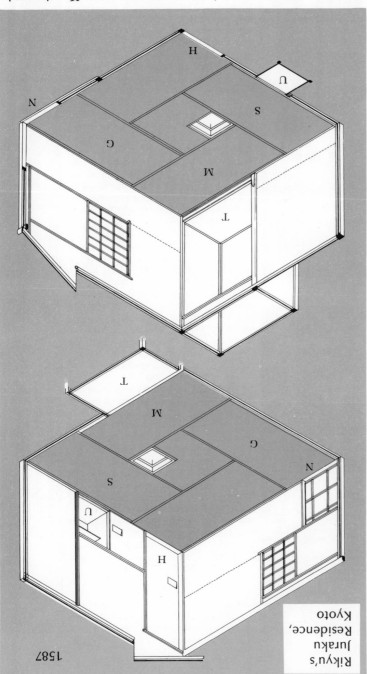

1587

1587

Rikyu's
Juraku
Residence,
Kyoto

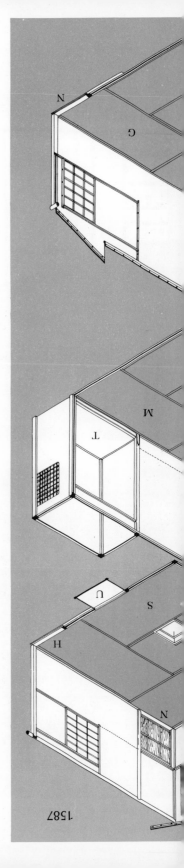

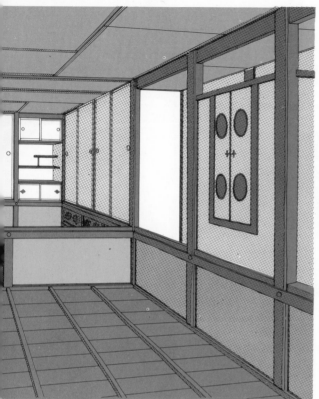

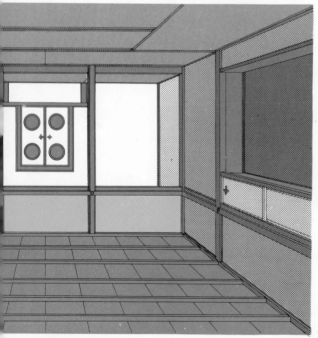

Jikinyu-ken Shoin and Anteroom, Ko

The following restoration drawings of three *shoin* and one tearoom designed by Enshu illustrate the originality and versatility of his style to a degree not seen in his extant works.

TAKINOMOTO-BO CHATATE-DOKORO (left, top). The Takimoto-bo in the Iwashimizu Hachiman Shrine, residence of Shokado Shojo, had a tearoom and several drawing rooms favored by Enshu. They were all destroyed by fire in 1773. The term *chatate-dokoro* means a *shoin* with tea-ceremony equipment. This room had a server's seat and a central post of bamboo to the left of the 6-*shaku* tatami tokonoma and, to its right, shelves and a *tsuke shoin*, forming a right angle. Opposite the latter, in the left wall, was a 6-*shaku* board-floor tokonoma. For the pattern of the openwork in the transom and the tokonoma-side panel, restoration drawings made by Horiguchi Sutemi have been consulted.

TAKINOMOTO-BO SHOIN (left, bottom). This diagram presents a view of the "lower room," nine mats in size, from the "higher room" of the *shoin* complex. Installed next to the veranda, at left, were the cupboards, and to their right, a server's seat fitted with an ingeniously arranged set of shelves. The tokonoma is set in the right-hand-side wall, with shelves that adjoin the "higher room."

JIKINYU-KEN SHOIN AND ANTEROOM (right). The present Jikinyu-ken does not belong to Enshu's age, but fortunately the stand-up paper models owned by the Koho-an and in Rakuo's collection transmit its appearance before the Koho-an burned down in 1793. According to them, although the present Bosen tearoom, also in the Koho-an, shows practically no change from the original, the Jikinyu-ken has changed considerably. The former Jikinyu-ken had a drawing room, the north end of which, measuring 12 *shaku*, was divided into three parts: a sanctuary in the center, flanked by tokonoma. Timbers with the bark left on were used for posts and the *nageshi* band encircling the room. The tokonoma also had *nageshi* at the same height, a method used also in the Bosen. The *tsuke shoin*, at left, had closets above it. The papered walls and the absence of windows recall the Mittan tokonoma, formerly a *tsuke shoin*. The anteroom, a 4.5-mat room with display shelves in one corner, is adjoined on the north side by a 3-mat tearoom. By removing all the sliding partitions the three rooms could be used as one room, and the *shoin* would take on the function of the "higher seat."

122. Tea bowl called Roku Jizo, formerly owned by Kobori Enshu. Ko-ido ware; diameter, 13.8 cm. Fifteenth or sixteenth century.

literary consciousness of beauty to the *wabi* tea.

Yet, if Enshu's tea was rich in variety, it was because the mood of the time demanded it, just as Oribe's taste had matched that of his age. What particularly influenced Enshu's utensils was the commercial exchange at the time with the Dutch and the Chinese. Though the age witnessed no flights of style such as those seen in the days of the Kitayama and Higashiyama periods, the imported ceramics and lacquerware suited the taste of the Japanese. The Aka-e porcelains with their red glaze and the simple blue-and-white Old Some-tsuke porcelains, both from China, as well as the ceramics from Holland—all these served to instill a fresh note of color in the utensils used at tea parties. At the same time, the local ceramic kilns located in different parts of the country acquired a new life. The effect of this fresh spirit was not limited merely to the kilns of certain restricted areas such as Mino, closely related to Oribe, or to those that produced the Iga and Bizen wares. A time had come, instead, in which tea utensils were baked in a wide variety of kilns in Seto, Kyoto, and Kyushu. When, during the Yi dynasty (1392–1910) in Korea, a guest mansion for the Japanese was established in Pusan, tea bowls in large numbers came to be baked in Korea on the basis of paper models sent by Enshu and others, leading inevitably to a proliferation of types. Enshu himself coped ambitiously with this rush for tea utensils. In keeping with his own taste he selected many works and added them as *chuko* (rediscovered) *meibutsu* to the categories of famous tea utensils dating from the times of Rikyu and Oribe and before. Leader in fact, as well as in name, he ruled over the world of tea of his time.

Among the works he selected as *chuko meibutsu* were the tea bowl named Roku Jizo (Fig. 122), a small Ido piece that he picked up at Roku Jizo in Fushimi; the Nagasaki Katade (Fig. 95), a Korean tea bowl with a thick blue-and-white glaze, owned at the time by Nagasaki Kyudayu; and the Osaka Marutsubo (Fig. 94), a tea caddy of Old Seto ware. The name of the last was chosen from a poem in

123. *Tea bowl called Oinami. Asahi ware; diameter, 13.2 cm. Seventeenth century.*

124. *Tea caddy called Ikuno. Tamba ware; height, 9 cm. First half of seventeenth century.*

the *Kokin-shu* and was intended to signify that the tea caddy, like the travelers' checkpoint called Osaka (a place near Kyoto, not the city on Osaka Bay), was of a character that he was unlikely to discover again.

One vivid illustration of the skill with which Enshu made famous objects of tea utensils is the way in which he selected tea caddies from Seto and other provincial kilns. The imaginary scenes suggested by the glazes and shapes were compared with scenes in the poems of the *Kokin-shu*, the *Shin Kokin-shu*, and other anthologies—hence the name Osaka Marutsubo, for example. In contrast with the matter-of-fact way of choosing names in the days of Rikyu and Oribe, Enshu's fashion was to add a literary element in the form of a poem title, thereby exciting the interest of men of *suki*. Moreover, his position as tea instructor to the shogun Iemitsu served very favorably to give greater authority to the *chuko meibutsu*. Many of the tea utensils in the collection of the third-generation lord of the Kaga fief, Maeda Toshitsune (1593–1658), were described as "coming from Enshu." That is, they were in the daimyo's collection upon Enshu's

own recommendation, and we can judge from this instance how great his authority was at the time.

If we look next at the setting for a tea party attended by Iemitsu on May 21, 1636, of the lunar calendar, and duly recorded in Enshu's tea records, we can find there a very clear reflection of the master's tea style.

In the room for the reception of the shogun, the tokonoma was decorated with a scroll bearing a poem by Fujiwara Teika (1160–1241) about falling cherry blossoms. On the upper level of the stand placed in front of the scroll was a red lacquer incense container in the shape of Hotei, the god of happiness, with a carved design of a bird; on the lower level, a golden incense burner shaped like a mythical lion. The other appointments of the room included "Rikyu's golden brazier," on which stood a kettle with a donkey design, and a utensil stand on which the following objects were placed: on the upper level, a tea caddy shaped like the neck of a crane and a *dai* (low, flat stand) of hibiscus design carrying a *yuteki temmoku* tea bowl, a tea ladle, a tea napkin, and a tea whisk; on the lower level, a bronze water jar.

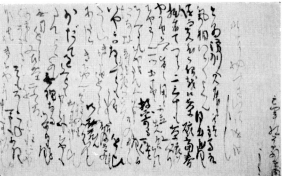

126. *Letter written by Kobori Enshu to the Confucian scholar Miyake Boyo. Ink on paper. First half of seventeenth century. Mitsui family, Tokyo.*

125. *Tea scoop called Kusemai, with case, by Kobori Enshu. First half of seventeenth century.*

The tokonoma in the Totomi (Enshu) tearoom was decorated with a scroll bearing the character for "moon" in the calligraphy of the Chinese priest Shih-ch'i (late Southern Sung) and a four-sided golden flower container with hollyhocks and white star lilies in it. On the brazier was a kettle with a flute design that had originally been sketched by the famous artist Kano Tan'yu (1602–74). The three shelves, on different levels, carried the following objects: on the top level, a small incense burner of blue celadon with a lion design and a mother-of-pearl incense container with a design of Hotei; on the middle level, a feather brush; on the bottom level, the Zaichu-an, a tea caddy of Seto ware. The earthenware *mizusashi* (water jar) was of gourd shape. For the tea bowls, Enshu chose Zeze ware. There was also a water jug of Takatori ware, together with a bamboo lid rest and a water ladle. On the veranda was a towel rack.

A third room, used for enjoying the cool of the day, had seating cushions and a three-tiered bamboo container for use in a flower-arrangement competition among the guests. The shogun himself created an arrangement of three hydrangeas.

As we have seen, in the tokonoma of the reception room Enshu hung an example of the calligraphy of the medieval poet Fujiwara Teika, and we should note that Teika's works were much in fashion at the time. On the stand in front of it he placed an incense container of multicoated red lacquer (*tsuishu*) and an incense burner of gold. The *yuteki temmoku* tea bowl mentioned among the decorations typified the collection of the Ashikaga shogunate from the time of the Eastern Hills Villa. In his choice of all these objects, as well as the others, Enshu sought a style in keeping with the authority of the shogun. Moreover, in his tearoom he acknowledged the presence of the shogun by placing hollyhocks in the square golden container, for the Tokugawa family crest consisted of three hollyhock leaves. For the other utensils, including the kettle, his favorite Zaichu-an tea caddy (a *meibutsu* of Old Seto ware), the three-level shelf, the water jar, and the tea bowls, he used only such as accorded with his own taste and connoisseurship, but he gave only a slight hint of his own tea style. In all this, his dignity is vividly revealed.

It is perhaps with some irony that Enshu's tea

127. Sunsho-an Shikishi, *attributed to Ki no Tsurayuki. Ink on* shikishi *paper; height, 13.4 cm.; width, 13 cm. About tenth century.*

128 (opposite page, left). Dutch incense ▷ *container in shape of a white wild goose. Height, 11.4 cm. Seventeenth century. Fujita Art Museum, Osaka.*

129 (opposite page, right). Jar with ▷ *wisteria design, by Nonomura Ninsei. Height, 28.8 cm. Second half of seventeenth century. Hakone Art Museum, Kanagawa Prefecture.*

style has been discussed here, but the power of his performance, which favored transcendence while all the time retaining its materialistic flavor, was in fact highly uncommon. What was visible on the surface, such as the variety of utensils and the abundance of color, as well as the literary expression, found warm welcome among the people of his time, in whose eyes his remarkable performance was reflected as *kirei sabi.*

THE NOSTALGIA FOR COURTLY ELEGANCE

Enshu's daimyo tea was carried on by Sekishu.

In the sphere of tea utensils, however, Sekishu lacked Enshu's talent, and beyond the refined and highly stylish tea caddies he left, nothing worth special mention remains. Enshu's *kirei-sabi* utensils could already be found in abundance in the repositories of daimyo and tea men, and thus Sekishu was left with practically nothing to accomplish. In any case he himself is thought not to have cared very much for employing utensils as showy exhibits.

One man whose tea offered a contrast with Enshu's was Kanamori Sowa, who developed an unconventional style of his own in Kyoto. His feeling for the rich, elegant beauty favored by the nobility —a feeling also disclosed in the appellation Hime Sowa—gives a clear idea of his taste.

The use of Teika's poems and of other old writings as alcove decorations began in the time of Jo-o, but it was in the Momoyama period that such works really came to be made much of, and the *Ogura Shikishi* (Fig. 98) had already been classified as *meibutsu* by the time of Toyotomi Hideyoshi. The works of calligraphy known by this name consisted of poems reputedly selected and transcribed by Teika on the large square cards called *shikishi.* Today only part of the original set survives.

About the middle of the seventeenth century, other old writings came to be highly prized, among them the *Sunsho-an Shikishi* (Fig. 127), which were once used as alcove decorations in the Sunsho-an teahouse of Sakuma Shogen (1570–1640), retainer of Tokugawa Ieyasu and governor of Kawachi

Province (Osaka), who on his retirement built this teahouse on the grounds of the Daitoku-ji. The poems on this set of *shikishi* had been beautifully transcribed on imported Chinese paper by the famous Heian-period poet Ki no Tsurayuki (868?– 945?), one of the compilers of the anthology *Kokin-shu*.

That such a trend was warmly encouraged among aristocratic tea circles in Kyoto is understandable. It was as though the tea favored by the imperial court were gradually taking definite shape around the nobility. In the years covering the second quarter of the seventeenth century, Kanamori Sowa built up warm friendships with Konoe Ozan, Ichijo Ekan, and Tofukumon-in, and it was in these circumstances that the world of Hime Sowa took shape.

Sowa's taste is symbolized by the representationally patterned Omuro pottery of Nonomura Ninsei, an artist whom we have already noted as a discovery of Sowa's. Under the guidance of Sowa, Ninsei produced many works expressive of the rich taste of the imperial court and at the same time created tea utensils to suit the taste of Tofukumon-in. As even a brief glance will show, these works have a graceful elegance befitting the Sowa style, and they faithfully reflect the preferences of the nobility. The pheasant incense burner of Figure 101 is a characteristic example of Ninsei's achievement. It is said that this work of art came into the possession of the Maeda daimyo family in Kaga Province upon Sowa's recommendation. Again, as in the instance of the Dutch incense container in the form of a white wild goose (Fig. 128), Sowa showed himself to have a keen feeling for refined works from Western countries as well. What is traditionally considered to be the Sowa taste, however, could perhaps be more correctly termed the taste of the Kyoto nobles in general rather than that of Sowa himself. But even the unpretentious and simply decorated Karatsu tea bowls that he selected and placed in his autographed "Sowa boxes" are beautiful in their own way—a point of great interest for what it reveals of the Sowa taste.

CHAPTER FIVE

Harmony, Respect, Purity, Tranquility

THE "BEGGAR" SOTAN When permission was granted to reinstate the Sen family, suppressed by Hideyoshi after Rikyu's death, Sen Sotan (also known as Gempaku; 1578–1658), grandson of Rikyu, and Sotan's father, Sen Shoan (1546–1614), moved Rikyu's residence from its location at Juraku-dai in Ichijo Yoshiya-cho to Ogawa-gashira, the site of the present Omote Senke school of tea. Sotan also strengthened the foundations of the Fushin-an teahouse and in his old age lived in retirement at the Konnichi-an. As recorded in the *Chawa Shigetsu Shu,* a collection of tea stories told by Fujimura Yoken (1613–99), a disciple of Sotan's, he led a simple life "indifferent throughout to riches and fame." In the *Hon'ami Gyojo Ki,* a record of the doings of Hon'ami Koetsu written by his grandson Hon'ami Koho, Sotan is spoken of as "my friend Sotan," and his life style had something in common with Koetsu's "aversion to catering to the tastes of those in power." Yet, insofar as Sotan attained *wabi* he undoubtedly surpassed Koetsu. His contemporaries knew him as Kojiki (Beggar) Sotan, in contrasting reference to Hime (Princess) Sowa, and in this slightly exaggerated metaphor are sounded the depths of *wabi.* It is questionable whether the *Zen Cha Roku* (Zen Tea Records) is really Sotan's posthumous work, as it is claimed, but the book does enable us

to know his way of serving tea and, besides, furnishes many other interesting hints. In this it deserves the same esteem as the writings about Rikyu in the *Nambo Roku.* The book focuses its attention on what it calls "the harmony of tea and Zen," and it belittles the tea centered on utensils, stressing instead the emergence of tea from the spirit of Zen. This was a premise later to take shape in the four concepts of harmony (*wa*), respect (*kei*), purity (*sei*), and tranquility (*jaku*). At the same time, however, Sotan had much of a graceful and courtly style of thinking, and he readily accepted the invitation to conduct a tea ceremony for a courtly figure of no less standing than Tofukumon-in, to whom he presented a first-class set of tea utensils. He also devised for the first time a red tea napkin for the ladies-in-waiting of the imperial palace, reputedly so that lipstick stains left on the tea bowl would not noticeably soil the napkin when they were rubbed off. This shows a hidden aspect of the "beggar" Sotan.

After Sotan's time the Sen family split up into three branches, thus opening the way for the advance of the *iemoto* (hereditary grand master) system. It was within this system that the ideas of harmony, respect, purity, and tranquility as related to the way of tea gradually took shape. Besides

130. The Seven Rites of the Sen School. Omote Senke school of tea, Kyoto.

taking note of this particular process, it is likewise important to consider the state of the tea ceremony at the time. We find, on doing so, that it was faced with two major problems. The first: how to harmonize its tendency to become just a recreation or a polite accomplishment with the religious sense inherent in Zen; the second: how to construct the *iemoto* system in the light of the new tea population that viewed tea as entertainment. The man who stood confronted with these problems was Joshinsai Tennen (1705–51), *iemoto* of the Omote Senke school.

While continuing to stress the religious ideal in *chado*, Joshinsai established seven grades of teaching that covered all the ground from beginner to master of tea. In addition he perfected a new form of *iemoto* system in which the *iemoto* reserved to himself the authority to award licenses. At the same time, between the years 1734 and 1751, in counsel with his younger brother Yugensai Itto of the Ura

Senke school, his disciple Kawakami Fuhaku (1716–1807; founder of the Fuhaku school), and others, he gradually came to recognize *chado* as a polite accomplishment. But in order to keep it within the bounds of moderation, he established as a kind of facilitating procedure the Senke Shichiji Shiki (Fig. 130), or Seven Rites of Tea, the group rituals performed by the participants of the *cha-no-yu*, each containing a principle to be observed in order to become a tea master. These were akin to the seven principles required for a master of Zen.

The four elements—harmony, respect, purity, and tranquility—did not from the outset form part of the spirit of the way of tea. It was at a time when the latter threatened to drift along aimlessly as a mere hobby that these elements were introduced to stop the drift by means of an all-out resistance— a barrier thrown up by those for whom tea was a way of Zen.

THE ''BEGGAR'' SOTAN · *125*

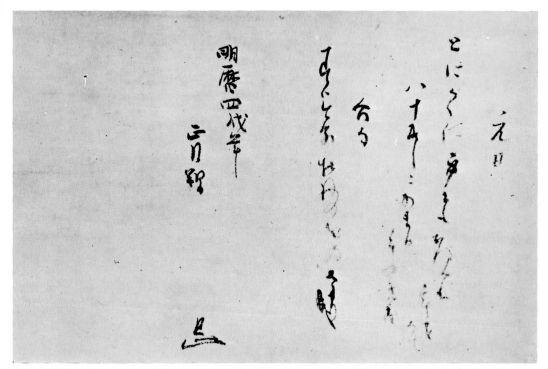

131. Shihitsu *(first writing of the new year)*, by Sen Sotan. *Ink on paper. 1658. Omote Senke school of tea, Kyoto.*

YORAKU-IN AND RATIONALISM

The tea drinking practiced in the merchant society at the beginning of the eighteenth century was not just an aimless entertainment. The merchants' view of life derived from a blending of wealth and amusement. Wealth was for the sake of amusement, one's life for the sake of wealth, and amusement for the sake of a fuller life. But their great accumulation of wealth was based on very careful planning, other than which they held to no idea or faith. To be rational was an imperative in all circumstances. In fact, in order for the tea ceremony to gain entry into merchant society it became necessary to provide rational explanations for its procedures, not merely to emphasize its spirituality.

The man who developed a concept of tea best fitted to such circumstances was Konoe Iehiro (1667–1738), who assumed the religious name Yoraku-in and who combined a firm grasp of courtly traditions with close friendships among the merchants, as, for example, with Konoike Do-oku (1655–1736). Born in a famous line of court regents, he was conversant with both Japanese and Chinese studies, knew poetry well, and was known as an excellent calligrapher in the style of the mid-Heian period. In a word, he was a typical man of the court. One of Oribe's disciples, he also studied tea under the tonsured imperial prince Kajiinomiya Jiin of the school of Hime Sowa. His tenets are revealed in detail in Yamashina Doan's *Kaiki*. There Yoraku-in sets out to explain rationally for his own personal satisfaction the various rules of *chado* in the light of its ultimate aim. It was just this kind of mentality that the merchant class found easy to accept, and Yoraku-in's thinking was destined to determine the direction taken from then on by the theories of *chado*—that

132. Calligraphy known as The Orthodox Line of Tea Masters. *Ink on paper. 1745. Kawakami family, Tokyo.*

is, to establish a rational foundation embodying the way of the Zen principles: harmony, respect, purity, and tranquility.

DEEPENING THE CONCEPT OF WABI It was Rikyu's second son, Shoan (1546–1614), who rehabilitated the Sen family on property located in front of the Hompo-ji temple in Kyoto. There he built the Zangetsu-tei (Figs. 38, 199), a *shoin* modeled on the 18-mat Colored Shoin of Rikyu's Juraku residence, and a 3-plus-a-*daime*-mat tearoom, also a reproduction of a tearoom of Rikyu's. In addition there was a 3-mat tearoom in the Doan-gakoi style originated by Rikyu's oldest son, Doan—that is, a tearoom equipped with a small enclosure for the host so that he could not be seen as he prepared the tea. In 1608, on the occasion of a visit by the rich merchant Matsuya from Nara, Sotan, who was then thirty years of age, used this room for serving tea. The purpose of the Doan-gakoi, or Doan enclosure, was to underline the modest attitude of the host, and as such it served Sotan well in view of his penchant for *wabi*. We do not know what subsequently became of this tearoom, but we do know that in 1615 Sotan revived Rikyu's 1.5-mat tearoom and named it the Fushin-an. In this typical Sen-family tearoom, this smallest of spaces used for tea—of whose original version it was said that "it is doubtful whether there is room in it for anyone besides Soeki"—there was already reflected the sternness of Sotan's decision to pursue *wabi* to its extreme limit.

Sotan gave greater depth to the *wabi* aspect of Rikyu's tea. For example, he carried Rikyu's *murodoko* style of tokonoma a step further in the direction of *wabi* by using clay instead of a tatami mat for its floor. To this new type of tokonoma he

133. Views of Fushin-an tearoom, showing server's seat (left) and host's entrance (right). Designed by Sen Sotan and remodeled by Sen Koshin, early seventeenth century; reconstructed in 1914. Omote Senke school of tea, Kyoto.

gave the name *tsuchidoko*, or clay tokonoma. The same aspiration toward *wabi* was displayed in his use of colors. Whereas Rikyu had cautioned that "objects thickly colored look vulgar and inferior," Sotan thought that "thick color is suitable for wood" and maintained that a ceiling of roughly woven bulrushes looked best colored black like soot, as we read in his tea record *Chafu*.

Sotan's son Koshin (or Sosa; 1619–72) expressed a wish to convert the Fushin-an, then a 1.5-mat room, to a 3-plus-a-*daime*-mat room, three mats placed side by side, with the *nijiri-guchi* at the narrow side of the mat farthest from the host's seat. Sotan gave his consent and cooperation, and the result was a model of the "room with a *daime*" typical of Rikyu's school (Fig. 133). As we can gather from his statement concerning the bamboo at the top and bottom of the extended wall that "the Rikyu school shall invariably employ bamboo, not wood," Sotan endeavored to set a standard for

the Rikyu school, even down to the smallest details. His motive was to resist the great vogue enjoyed at the time by the styles of Oribe, Enshu, and Sowa.

On his retirement, Sotan built a 2-mat room (the Konnichi-an; Fig. 147) and also a 4.5-mat room (the Yu-in; Figs. 73, 148, 187, 191). The latter seems to have been copied from Rikyu's 4.5-mat room at his Juraku residence. It has only two windows besides the skylight, and the atmosphere of seeking for truth is well sustained by the ample wall space and the low ceiling. The device of using a corner post visible only at the top—a *yoji-bashira*, or toothpick post, as it is called—greatly enhances the *wabi* effect.

Sotan's style of tea deeply infiltrated the powerful merchant class. The Shitenno, or Four Famous Disciples of Sotan—Fujimura Yoken (1613–99), Sugiki Fusai (1628–1706), Yamada Sohen (1627–1708), and Miyake Boyo (1580–1649), who all

134. View of Kanden-an teahouse. About 1790. Arisawa family, Shimane Prefecture.

135. Traveling Poet Li Po, by Liang K'ai. Ink on paper; height, 80.9 cm.; width, 30.3 cm. Southern Sung dynasty, twelfth or thirteenth century. Tokyo National Museum.

136 (opposite page, top). Calligraphy ▷ by Yuan-wu K'o-ch'in known as Nagare Engo. Certificate of authorization for teaching Zen. Ink on paper; height, 43.9 cm.; width, 52.1 cm. Northern Sung dynasty, about 1124. Tokyo National Museum.

137 (opposite page, bottom). Chinese ▷ bunrin (apple-shaped) tea caddy called Honno-ji. Ming dynasty, fifteenth or sixteenth century. Goto Art Museum, Tokyo.

首祖□未惟務單傳直指不喜帶一水拖泥打露布列
窠窟鈍置人盖擇迦老子三万條會對機設撥立世諦
築大段周遮是故最後徑截省要後最上機雖白迦葉
以八萬少示機開多顯理致王末付受三除靡不直面提持如
倒剎竿盡氷設針示回光相軋赤幟把明鑑訟如鐵橛
子�′佐偈達靈覽破六宗與道真義天下太平幸輳我天尔
鈞峇神機迓權那疑作兩側涸到泉游觀光後顯
言敎外別行通宗通歷世说久具正眼大解脫宗師寶
大鑒逹逢佛不眾名相不虖理性言说放出活卓地脫灑
革通逹逢佛不眾名相不虖理性言说放出活卓地脫灑
自由出機遠見非傳行明以章述言以機雜機以毒攻
毒以用碡用两以流傳上百末年故知派別各種家風
浩…車轟莫知絕然籲其歸嗜無出直指人心心
既明無此竟邁矣如揚安穩之場些者二發我示謂百川異派
到大体大歇安穩且不而上根器其是為誠遠見百川歸
同歸于海要頂我是非知見解金逹
佛祖志氣然後能保入處微在信得真下把
得住如何可即證堪兮種草撿此切直賨秋慎訶勿
作容易敬行也

雨
花
雲
肺
欽
長
沙

陵
々
殘
虹
紫
晚
霞

最
好
市
橋
發
柳
升

酒
旗
搖
曳
尋
思
家

138. Mountain Village in a Fine Haze by Yu-chien. One of a set of eight hand scrolls entitled Eight Views c
of the Hsiao and the Hsiang. Ink on paper; height, 33 cm.; length, 84 cm. Southern Sung dynasty, twelfth c
hirteenth century. Yoshikawa family, Tokyo.

alled Hosokawa.

世臨多巇隂
無思不研竆
平生見稿老
今日自戍箱
愳字眠猶從
及諢亙者籠
信天川直道
休問馬牛風
日本照禪者
故淂牧字径
川述嘗贈之
靈堂叟 書

140. *Section of Buddhist sermon written by Hsu-t'ang Chih-yu. Ink on paper; height, 28.5 cm.; length, 71.5 cm.*
Southern Sung dynasty, twelfth or thirteenth century. Tokyo National Museum.

141. *Tea bowl called Kizaemon. O-ido ware; diameter, 15.4 cm. Yi dynasty, fifteenth or sixteenth century. Koho-an,*
Daitoku-ji, Kyoto.

142. Interior view of Kogetsu-tei teahouse. About 1790. Arisawa family,
Shimane Prefecture.

143. View of tea garden, showing steppingstone path and tsukubai (low stone basin). About 1797–1800. Koho-an, Daitoku-ji, Kyoto.

144. Interior view of
Seiko-ken tearoom.
1863. Seison-kaku,
Ishikawa Prefecture.

145. *Views of Yodomi no Seki teahouse, showing* nijiri-guchi *(left) and server's seat viewed from guests' seats (right). Designed by Fujimura Yoken. About 1685. Saio-in, Kyoto.*

inherited his style and sought to propagate it—achieved remarkable results in their designing of tearooms and tea gardens, in their literary works, and in their other creative activities. In his later years Fujimura Yoken built a 3-mat Doan-gakoi tearoom at the Saio-in subtemple of the Komyo-ji at Kurodani in Kyoto (Fig. 145). He provided it with a *murodoko* and an open-timbered ceiling, the result being an expression of *wabi* closely akin to that of his master, Sotan. It seems that Yoken also had a hand in creating the *wabi* atmosphere of the Tennenzue-tei, a *shoin*-style teahouse that today forms part of the Izome residence at Katada in the city of Otsu, Shiga Prefecture.

The celebrated artist Ogata Korin (1658–1716), who is said to have studied tea under Zuiryusai (1660–1701), the fifth-generation grand master of the Omote Senke school, had a profound knowledge of tearooms, and stand-up paper models that

he designed have been handed down to the present day. His mansion at Shimmachi in Osaka was so skillfully planned around the theme of tea that its design could be taken for that of a tea master. In all likelihood, Korin also took part in the planning of the Shusei-do hermitage in Omuro, residence of his younger brother the famous potter Kenzan (1663–1743). The Ryokaku-tei teahouse (Fig. 150), which can be seen today at the Ninna-ji temple, is thought to have been part of the Shusei-do, and even now it retains the feeling for design that characterized the Genroku-era merchants at the turn of the seventeenth century.

THE RELAXATION OF SPATIAL TENSION

After Sotan's time the Senke (Sen family) style of tea went through a long period of stagnation. Eventually, however, from the time of Kakukakusai (1678–1730), sixth-

146. *Inner gate in garden of Kankyu-an teahouse, in the style of Mushanokoji Sen Jikisai (d. 1782). Rebuilt about 1926. Mushanokoji Senke school of tea, Kyoto.*

147. *Interior view of Konnichi-an tearoom, designed by Sen Sotan. Originally built in 1648; rebuilt in late eighteenth century. Ura Senke school of tea, Kyoto.*

generation grand master of Omote Senke, the style acquired a new look, and it gradually began to flourish again. Kakukakusai favored the type of tearoom that employed an Uraku-gakoi, an enclosure closely resembling the Doan-gakoi, and is said to have been the originator of two new styles of tokonoma: the *genso-doko*, a three-quarter-mat tokonoma of *daime* size, and the *masu-doko*, a half-mat, square-shaped tokonoma. He thereby introduced changes of design in the hitherto spiritually oriented style of tearoom construction. Since the Rikyu school of tea could no longer survive within the truth-seeking context alone, the masters sought new forms of expression in the tearoom that would blend with the mood of the times. Kakukakusai's successor, Joshinsai, seventh-generation grand master of Omote Senke, further propelled this tendency forward.

During the early 1740s, Konoike Ryoei of Osaka built a mortuary chapel at the Gyokurin-in subtemple of the Daitoku-ji and named it the Nammyo-an. It included a tearoom and a *shoin*, and we are told that the building and its tea garden were admired by Joshinsai, with whom Ryoei was friends. It is thought that the arrangement of the rooms, with the chapel in the center and the Sa-an tearoom (Fig. 72) and the *shoin* Kasumi-doko no Seki (Fig. 103) on either side of it, was designed to permit the holding of a Buddhist service in the form of a tea ceremony. The *shoin* features a tokonoma whose staggered shelves (*chigaidana*) suggest trailing mist (*kasumi*) and thus give it the name *kasumi-doko*, or mist tokonoma.

The interior of the Sa-an, as can be imagined from its rustic and typically Rikyu-school exterior, displays at first glance a rather severe spatial com-

148. Interior view of Yu-in tearoom, designed by Sen Sotan. Nijiri-guchi *viewed from server's seat. Originally built in 1653; rebuilt in late eighteenth century. Ura Senke school of tea, Kyoto.*

position. The scarcity of windows and the extent to which light is restrained clearly show a strict adherence to the rules observed ever since Rikyu's time. But a number of the other features of the room just as clearly show a relaxation of the spatial composition. The three-mat area has been enlarged by the insertion of a section of wooden floor (*naka-ita*). The ceiling is of three different levels, one of which comprises a dropped ceiling. The hearth is located off center in relation to the server's seat, and consequently the rather frail center post, which is distinguished by a strong curve, is also off center and does not stand at the point where the ceilings over the server's mat and the guests' mats intersect. All these features illustrate quite well the tendency of the times to seek pleasure in visual variations rather than in spatial tension.

We can find further evidence of the trend of the times in the Kan'in no Seki tearoom at the Juko-in subtemple of the Daitoku-ji. Here Joshinsai created a structure of superb balance and stability and thereby left us proof that he himself was a man who had a firm grasp of tearoom design.

The mention of a 4.5-mat room with a 6-*shaku* tokonoma, papered walls, and a coffered ceiling conjures up the image of a rather austere *shoin*-style room. Yet this is by no means the case with the Kasumi-doko no Seki. Here such devices as the use of bamboo in place of the customary wooden *nageshi* band and of smoked bamboo at the outer edge of the tokonoma floor have brought about a fusion of the *soan* and the *shoin*. And this, for a man accustomed to building tearooms in the *soan* style, was truly an original idea for the *shoin*. The insertion of staggered shelves across the full width of the tokonoma was a bold concept, understand-

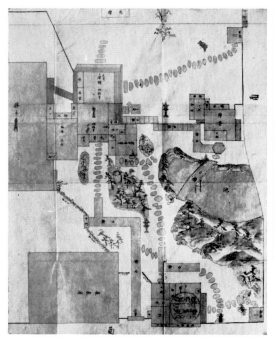

150. *View of Ryokaku-tei teahouse. Originally built about 1688; relocated between 1843 and 1880. Ninna-ji, Kyoto.*

149. *Plan of Shusei-do, retreat of Ogata Kenzan, before Ryokaku-tei teahouse was removed. From* Shosho Sukiya Ezu *(Illustrations of Various Sukiya) by Nakai Shusui. Nakane family, Kyoto.*

ably difficult for tea masters to accept at first. In the merchant society of the eighteenth century, however, such designs were expected as a matter of course. When tea reached the stage at which it could pass for both a "way" and an entertainment, the aesthetic standards of the way of tea, even in structural design, began to waver mightily.

IN THE SPACE OF just eighty years, beginning in 1573, four outstanding tea men made their appearance, separated from one another by periods of about twenty years. They were Rikyu, Oribe, Enshu, and Sowa. This was surely one of the lucky accidents of history, which in the course of its long march has seldom witnessed such a sin-

gular occurrence. It is no overstatement to say that the tea cult came to play a central role in Japan's cultural history because of the outstanding support and guidance it received at crucial moments in its development.

Looking back from a present-day perspective, one gets the impression that the aesthetic criteria of the world of tea have been determined almost entirely on the basis of the various styles of *furyu* shown by these four men. Every "good form," including such aspects as introversion and extroversion, stillness and movement, lack of individuality and display of individuality, absence of taste and colorful display of taste, absence of creative originality and presence of creative originality—in a

151. Buddhist poem written by Sen Sotan on his deathbed. Ink on paper. 1658. Ura Senke school of tea, Kyoto.

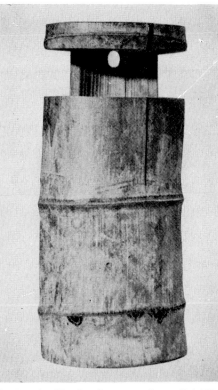

152. One-tiered bamboo flower container called Hibiki (Echo), by Sen Sotan.

word, all that can be expected from the tea world —came into existence in the space of these eighty years. Accordingly, nearly all the outstanding works of art known today in tea may be said to have had their aesthetic value determined in the interval of these men's lives. Naturally, though, since this value was ultimately sought within the standard of "beauty, namely function," these works of art fail on some counts to convince us when we view them in the light of today's standards based on the inherent quality of the work. Yet, if we stop to consider how great has been the influence of the four tea masters' peculiar brand of aesthetic awareness on the Japanese standard of beauty, there can then remain no doubt in our minds that the achievements of these men deserve our special appraisal.

FAVORITE TEA UTENSILS OF SOTAN

While Enshu, as a versatile "stage producer," was devoting himself to the daimyo tea, and Sowa, living for the elegant tea of the nobles, was absorbed in the creation of a new style, it was Sen Sotan alone who endeavored to devote his life to *wabi* tea: the fusion of tea and Zen. In Rikyu's case, to live for *wabi* tea had been largely an idea out of touch with daily life, whereas Sotan made living in poverty his creed and attempted to penetrate to the very heart of the Zen tenet "Man originally possesses nothing."

154. *Lacquer tea caddy in the style of Sen Sotan. First half of seventeenth century.*

153. *Top: tea bowl called Amadera (Nunnery), by Tanaka Chojiro. Black Raku ware; diameter, 9.8 cm. Bottom: its box, with inscription by Sen Sotan. Sixteenth or seventeenth century. Tokyo National Museum.*

155. *Tea bowl called Koshin, formerly owned by Sen Koshin. Ko-ido ware; diameter, 13.7 cm. Yi dynasty, fifteenth or sixteenth century. Hatakeyama Museum, Tokyo.*

156. *Section of a set of fifteen poems in the calligraphy of Fujiwara Teika. Ink on* kaishi *paper. Thirteenth century.*

In the tea world of Sotan the creative originality and "stage production" of Oribe, Enshu, and Sowa became totally unnecessary, and for this reason his choice of tea utensils, too, showed a deep taste for those that displayed no artifice in their making. His tea bowls were the bowls of Chojiro and the unassuming Ido bowls of Korea; his water jars were of Shigaraki and Bizen ware; his flower containers, of bamboo; and in the tokonoma he hung calligraphic scrolls. Such preferences indicate a taste that had achieved *wabi*.

Moreover, unlike Enshu and Sowa, Sotan did not handle tea utensils as objects intended primarily to achieve some stage effect but sought rather to comprehend the inner meaning of each separate bowl. He gave names to quite a number of Chojiro tea bowls and inscribed the boxes in which they were kept. The significance of the names and the manner of his *hakogaki*, or box inscriptions, contrast sharply with what we find in the case of Enshu, whose use of classical Teika-style writing on a fine box seemed intended to proclaim the quality of the utensil inside. Sotan wrote his *hakogaki* in a carefree and unaffected style, expressing what he felt upon reaching a sympathy with the inner feeling of the bowl itself. This attitude reveals the extreme refinement of a man of *furyu* who sought to live the *wabi* spirit, and it is indeed an engaging one. In this sense, it can perhaps be said that Sotan's *hakogaki,* more than those of any other tea man, were as *hakogaki* really should be.

He also had lacquerware tea caddies, water jars, and tea bowls made to suit his own taste. While in line with the taste of Rikyu, Doan, and Shoan, these utensils were further infused with the feeling of *wabi* that Sotan gave them, thus taking him one

157. *Hexagonal dish with design of god of longevity, by Ogata Kenzan and Ogata Korin. Longer diameter, 27.1 cm.; shorter diameter, 24 cm. Late seventeenth century. Okura Cultural Foundation, Tokyo.*

158. *Kinrande (gold-decorated) water vessel. Height, 21.2 cm. Ming dynasty, sixteenth century. Konoike family, Osaka.*

step further than his predecessors had gone. Typical of his taste were the sober, rough-textured *ikkambari* lacquerware tea caddies and flower containers made of bamboo, and he particularly liked them. Sotan, it may be confidently said, was the one tea master who lived the *wabi* ideal both in spirit and in deed.

UTENSILS OF YORAKU-IN'S TIME
As the eighteenth century got under way, an age grown mature tended no longer to rest content with the *wabi* tea of Sotan. This was especially true in the case of tea utensils. The transition was to a world in which there emerged a multitude of outstanding wares somewhat like the profuse blossoming of a multitude of flowers. To the utensils of the Higashiyama

and the Momoyama ages were added those newly made and fancied in the days of Enshu and Sowa, and now, with the entry into the Edo period (1603–1868), also those brought over from China—the so-called *watarimono* (imported goods). Among these, the late Ming products of the mid-seventeenth century, were *kinrande* (Figs. 106, 158), a rough gold-painted porcelain for general use; the blue-and-white Old Sometsuke (Figs. 96, 194); the Shonzui, of a violet hue; and the roughly designed red-decorated Nanking Aka-e.

These were times, moreover, when the wealth of the merchants was making itself felt, and once again tea utensils found favor as items for collection. Merchants of extreme wealth figured actively as lovers of tea utensils. And among these men were Yodoya Tatsugoro of Osaka, active during the

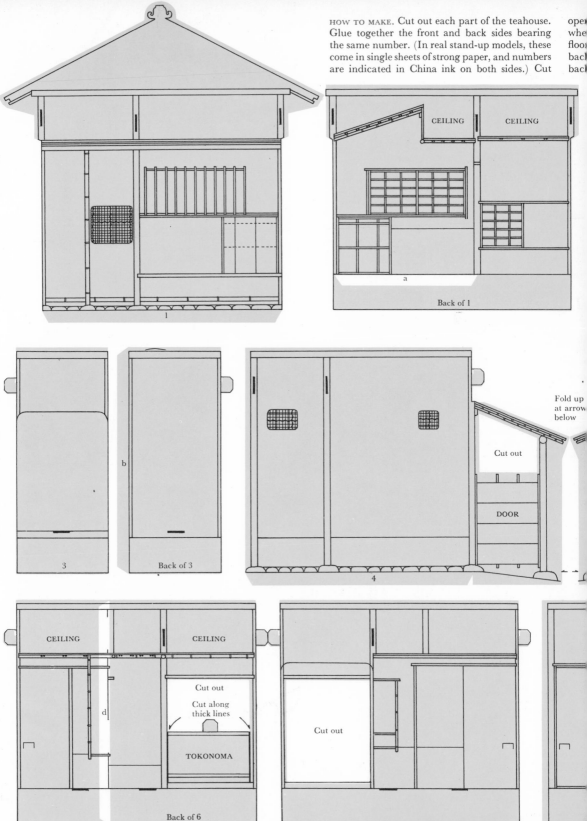

HOW TO MAKE. Cut out each part of the teahouse. Glue together the front and back sides bearing the same number. (In real stand-up models, these come in single sheets of strong paper, and numbers are indicated in China ink on both sides.) Cut ope— whe— floo— bac— bac—

CEILING   CEILING

a

Back of 1

b

3   Back of 3

4

Fold up at arrow below

Cut out

DOOR

CEILING   CEILING

Cut out
Cut along thick lines

d

TOKONOMA

Cut out

Back of 6

6

the slots for inserting the tabs. Apply glue indicated (a–j). Glue the 2-mat tearoom to the back of 1; 1-mat anteroom floor to the of 4; 1-mat preparation-room floor to the of 7; the single shelf to the back of 5; the three-level shelf to the front of 8; 3 to the back of 2; 5 to the back of 6; 8 to the back of 7. Glue 1, 2, 3, 4, 6, and 7 to the corresponding numbers on the floor plan. Stand each of them up, insert tabs into slots, and model will be made.

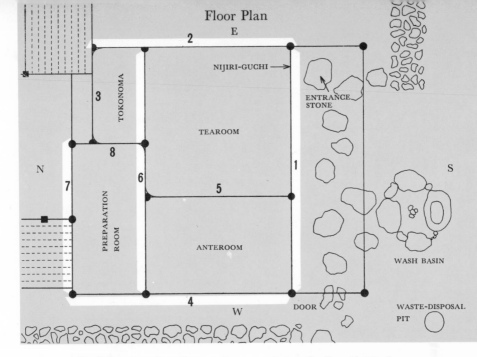

Floor Plan

E

2

NIJIRI-GUCHI

TOKONOMA

3

NIJIRI-GUCHI

ENTRANCE STONE

TEAROOM

8

N

6

7

5

1

S

PREPARATION ROOM

ANTEROOM

WASH BASIN

4

W

DOOR

WASTE-DISPOSAL PIT

a

Foldout 3: Stand-up Model of Tai-an

The stand-up paper model, a device for realizing a three-dimensional form by erecting walls on the ground paper, unites the drawings of the floor plan and elevations in one system. When this method was originated is not known, but tea masters have made ample use of it. To express the complexity of the three-dimensional structure of the teahouse, there was no other way. In the generous use they made of this method, we can see how seriously the tea masters have been concerned with effective spatial structure. The diagram of the Tai-an, found in Rakuo's collection, conveys its mid-Edo-period appearance, the direction of the roof and location of the windows being different from the present ones. Here, the roof has been corrected to match its present condition, and the floors, of tatami mats, have been added.

PREPARATION ROOM

7

8

3

6

SHELF

5

TOKO-NOMA

2

4

ANTEROOM

TEAROOM

1

HOW TO FOLD. Fold the mats and shelves upward; fold down 7, 6, and 1 in this order to the north and 4, 5, and 2 to the west. The whole structure will then be flat. It can be reassembled easily when required.

The tabs of a stand-up model are usually notched as in the above illustration. Such details as this are omitted here.

How to Assemble

Genroku era (1688–1704); Konoike Do-oku, also of Osaka; and Fuyuki Kaheiji, a mid-Edo timber merchant.

There was also Konoe Yoraku-in, the nobleman who lived the life of an aristocrat of artistic refinement. As stated in the *Kaiki*, his tea style symbolized that of his age. He enjoyed drinking tea with a wide variety of people that included tea men of the stature of Hisada Soya, fourth-generation grand master of the Hisada school, and the merchant Konoike Do-oku, as well as the court nobles. With a freedom of spirit undeterred by tradition and with no bias toward the old or the new, he devised arrangements that pleased him, and in this his handling of every variety of tea utensil was masterful. Such was the wellborn and well-bred aristocrat Konoe Yoraku-in.

An event of interest took place at the tea party on November 10, 1725, of the lunar calendar. At this gathering, as plates for the *kaiseki* meal, Yoraku-in used what were referred to as "Kenzan wares," the wares of Ogata Kenzan, who, some two decades earlier, in 1703, had begun to make pottery at Narutaki in Kyoto. In a word, for Yoraku-in any utensil was suitable if he could use it with enjoyment. In his day, unlike that of Yamanoue Soji before him, the manner and taste in tea utensils centered on other than prescribed patterns.

CHAPTER SIX

The Taste for Renowned Wares

FACED WITH THE rising prosperity of the merchant class newly emerging in the early eighteenth century, the shogunate reacted. By effecting the Kyoho (1716–36) reforms, which spanned most of the period of rule of the eighth Tokugawa shogun, Yoshimune (1684–1751), it succeeded in bringing pressure to bear on that prosperity and likewise in bolstering the feudal system. The movements of men of this time like Joshinsai of the Sen family can be understood when viewed as reactions to these reforms. Later the shoguns were obliged to carry out the reforms of Kansei (1787–93), undertaken by Matsudaira Sadanobu (1758–1829), one of Yoshimune's grandsons, and those of Tempo (1841–43), undertaken by Mizuno Tadakuni (1793–1851), titular governor of Echizen Province (present Fukui Prefecture). These reforms in turn influenced the clan governments in various provinces.

The Kansei reforms, in particular, brought about the restoration of wise rulers in various fiefs. The strengthening of clan governments was aimed at increasing industry and production and providing relief for the destitute. It so happened that the wise rulers responsible for the implementation of these reforms were also outstanding tea men. The leading figures in the Kansei reforms included Matsudaira Sadanobu, lord of the Shira-

kawa clan in northern Japan, who upon his retirement adopted the tea name Rakuo, and the lords Tokugawa Haruyasu of Mito, Matsudaira Yoshiaki of Echizen, and Matsudaira Fumai of Matsue. One feature common to these wise rulers and tea men, reflecting the state of the utensil repositories formerly filled with important wares but now empty on account of the poverty among the clans, was their strict opposition to the amassing of rare utensils. The "Enlightened Lord of Mito" (Tokugawa Haruyasu) advocated a return to the spirit of Rikyu, declaring, as recorded in the *Mito no Kinen* (Chronicles of Mito Clan), that "to be engrossed in collecting rare utensils deserves contempt."

MATSUDAIRA FUMAI Matsudaira Fumai (1751–1818) was the seventh-generation clan lord of Matsue in Izumo Province (present Shimane Prefecture) and in that capacity achieved outstanding results for the fief government. Introduced to the way of tea in the school of Enshu, he later became a disciple of the Isa branch of the Sekishu school. When no more than twenty years of age, he was initiated into the method of the formal style of tea using the *daisu*, and he also practiced Zen under the abbot Daiten of the Tenshin-ji temple at Azabu

159. Vicinity of Matsue Castle, where Matsudaira Fumai resided. Shimane Prefecture.

in Edo, receiving the Buddhist name Fumai. Reaching deep into the mysteries of tea while still a young man, he harshly criticized the way in which the tea ceremony was generally practiced at the time. In 1770, at the age of nineteen, he wrote the *Mudagoto* (Idle Words), an essay concerning *chado*. Taking up in it the didactic poem by Rikyu "It is foolish to desire many utensils / when with one kettle alone tea can be served," Fumai maintained that the *cha-no-yu* for the sake of utensils lacked moral principle and that the true *cha-no-yu* was the way to "the cultivation of the person, the regulation of the family, the ordering well of the state, and the making tranquil of the whole world." Such, at the time of his youth, were his frank thoughts concerning tea.

And yet, as the governing of his fief gradually came to achieve success, he too, while continuing to advocate strongly the revival of ethical tea,

began to devote time to the collection of rare utensils. This modification of his ideas sprang from the results achieved in efforts to increase industry and production and strengthen his fief's internal defenses, as well as from the remarkable successes achieved by the system of his government and the financial wealth built up by the fief. At the same time, however, it cannot be dismissed just as a taste for valuable antiques that he, with all his wealth, was in a position to purchase. The very fact that his taste for *meibutsu* evolved after his period of sweeping criticism of the collecting of famous wares would, alone, have induced in him a different attitude.

He gathered together masterpieces from all over the country, such as Mu-ch'i's *Returning Sails on a Vast Bay* (Fig. 169) and the Aburaya Katatsuki (Fig. 168), a high-shouldered tea caddy from China owned by the wealthy merchant Aburaya

160. Arare *(hailstone-patterned) teakettle called* Onjo-ji, *formerly owned by Matsudaira Fumai. Old* Ashiya ware; *iron. Sixteenth century. Tokyo National Museum.*

of Sakai, and his pride in them is revealed in the pages of the *Unshu Kura Cho* (Records of the Izumo Province Repository), a catalogue of his collection of tea utensils in Izumo, where he ruled as daimyo. Yet underlying this collecting of Fumai's was his attitude of research that prompted him to deal with the utensils insofar as they were objects of art. Here the collecting of *meibutsu* becomes meaningful for the first time through research. In the 1790s, under the pseudonym Old Man Tosai Shoko, he completed the eighteen-volume work *Kokon Meibutsu Ruiju* (Classified Collection of Renowned Wares of Ancient and Modern Times), an explanation of tea-utensil masterpieces such as *o-meibutsu* (famous before Rikyu's time), *meibutsu* (famous in Rikyu's time), and *chuko meibutsu* (selected by Enshu) from old times up until his day. Then in 1811, at the age of sixty, he compiled the three volumes of *Seto Toki Ransho* (Origins of Seto Ware). In yet another

book, *Chaso* (Foundations of Tea), an outline of the basic principles governing tea parties, he expounded his views on tea during the closing years of his life. The opinions he expressed here represent a comprehensive outlook on tea, symbolized in his statement that "the system of every school shall be mine." His ability was amply demonstrated not only in these works but also in his tearooms and tea gardens. In consequence, his career may be termed the crowning point of the history of tea in recent times.

SIGNS OF THE AP-
PROACHING MEIJI
RESTORATION

At the outset of the Tempo reforms Japan was faced with mounting pressure from abroad on the northern and southern fronts, while within the nation itself the capitalistic expansion of a merchandise economy was progressing and a growing

161. *View of Kogetsu-tei teahouse. 1792. Arisawa family, Shimane Prefecture.*

crisis threatened the feudal system. For the shogunate, the only way left open was to encourage a conservative policy of simplicity and frugality, the promotion of the martial arts, and the return of migrant farmers to their own villages—a policy that was quite unwelcome to the way of tea. In the powerful clans of southwestern Japan—Satsuma, Nagato, and Saga—efforts were made to control the production of goods and the circulation of money and to pour profits back into the clan economy. This naturally affected the production of ceramics, as in the case of wares from the fief kilns of Nabeshima, the Gosambutsu ware of Hagi, and the *oniwa* ware of Satsuma, the last mentioned consisting of utensils baked at the clan castles and mansions during the Edo period. In Echizen, great care was taken in the production of tea. Tokugawa Nariaki (1800–60), lord of the Mito clan, Matsudaira Yoshinaga (1828–90) of Echizen, and others

—the wise rulers and tea men of the era of the Tempo reforms—became the reformist group in the union of powerful clans that marked the Ansei era (1854–60).

In reaction to the policies and activities of these men, Ii Naosuke (1815–60), lord of Hikone, who, as leader of the faction that sought to preserve the dictatorial powers of the shogun, had risen to the position of great elder, sought to maintain the shogunate and the feudal system in order to further his ideal of absolute shogunal authority. To this end he resolutely enforced the breaking down of Japan's national isolation by the conclusion of commercial treaties, a step he saw as perfectly logical. Criticized by some as a conservative politician and praised by others as a pioneer for bringing to an end the isolation of his country, Naosuke, on this momentous occasion in Japanese history, put his convictions to the test. No doubt he acquired his

162. Cha-no-yu Ichi-e Shu, a book on the tea ceremony by Ii Naosuke. 1859. Ii Tairo Memorial Hall, Shiga Prefecture.

courageous spirit and logical mind from the discipline of Zen and tea. His tea name was Sokan.

While he was engaged in the study of tea in the Sekishu school, Naosuke, by way of the *Nambo Roku,* found himself holding many ideas in common with Rikyu, Nambo Sokei, and Tachibana Jitsuzan (1655–1708), founder of the Nambo school. He himself founded the Sokan school, as a branch of the Sekishu school, and in time published the *Cha-no-yu Ichi-e Shu* (Fig. 162), an explanation of all kinds of *cha-no-yu* rules. Two of his statements in the book are widely known: "Each encounter with a guest should be treated as if it were the last in a lifetime" and "After a tea party, sit alone and think." The concept conveyed by the first of these statements expresses forcefully both the mutual good will of host and guest and the harmony in the arrangement of the utensils.

Included among the many famous utensils comprising the household treasures of the Ii family were *o-meibutsu* like the Miyao Katatsuki, a high-shouldered tea caddy once owned by Miyao Daifu. At the same time, Naosuke himself made utensils for which he showed an outstanding feeling. Without neglecting to encourage the Koto ware of his own fief kilns, he strove continually to create new utensils. In this respect, as well as in others, he ranks side by side with Matsudaira Fumai as a wise ruler and tea man.

THE SUKIYA   The statement by Sen Koshin that "what is called a *sukiya* today bears no resemblance whatever to a *sukiya*" indicates that teahouses of the mid-seventeenth century, disregarding the standards of the classical teahouse (or tearoom) and inclining toward the expression of

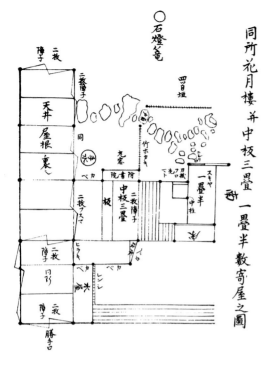

163. Plan of Kagetsu-ro pavilion and tearoom, in the style of Kawakami Fuhaku.

164. Interior view of Kanden-an tearoom, showing server's seat. 1793. Arisawa family, Shimane Prefecture.

worldly tastes, had developed into structures popularly known as *sukiya* even though they had no right to the name. In brief, the word *sukiya*, or teahouse, had taken on a new meaning. The facile popularization and the resulting confusion of teahouse designs were beyond doubt unacceptable to orthodox tea masters, but the new *sukiya* continued in its popularity, thereby hastening the classical teahouse along the road to deterioration. The sense of creativity retreated, to be replaced by set forms, and as the *sukiya* advanced in popularity, original teahouse standards were lost sight of. The man who adopted an attitude of resistance in the face of this architectural crisis in the world of tea was Kawakami Fuhaku, a leading disciple of Joshinsai's and a tireless promoter of the Senke style of tea in Edo. At his training school in Edo he revived a style of building suitable for the Seven Rites of Tea, calling it the Kagetsu-ro (Fig. 163), and along with it an orthodox Sen-style tearoom. It was at this point that Matsudaira Fumai made his appearance, and the freedom of his style, breaking out of the stagnation in which tea had bogged down, attracted widespread attention.

THE OVERTHROW OF FIXED FORMS

The retreat built by Fumai in his late years stood on a high plateau overlooking Shinagawa in Edo and was called the Osaki-en. Comprising more than ten buildings, including a mansion, a *sukiya*, and teahouses, it was the legacy of Fumai that deserved more than any other to be treasured. Yet in 1849 it was mercilessly torn down on orders from the shogunate. Fortunately, drawings of the buildings of the Osaki-en have been preserved, and they give us an idea of what the

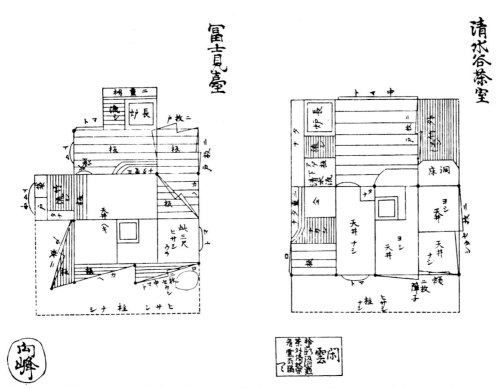

165. *Plans of Koho teahouse at Fujimidai (left) and Kan'un teahouse at Shimizudani (right) in Osaki-en retreat of Matsudaira Fumai. From* Chado Hokan *(Handbook of the Way of Tea).*

buildings were like. Among them is the drawing of a teahouse called the Koho no On-chashitsu (Fig. 165), which stood on top of a rise called the Fuji-midai, or Plateau for Viewing Mount Fuji.

The teahouse is centered on a 2.5-mat room with a *mizuya* adjoining the server's seat and has triangular sections of flooring integrated with the wooden-floored veranda to produce an interestingly patterned composition. (The *mizuya* consists of a set of shelves, a sink, and a number of small cabinets and is used for washing and storing the tea utensils and other items.) This teahouse displays an unconventional technique that sought to break down the established patterns. In Fumai this is not surprising, for he maintained forcefully that "to be a slave to convention and therefore get tangled in the web of principles is suffocating."

At the villa of the Arisawa family, whose ancestors were the chief retainers of Matsue, in Shimane Prefecture, there is a teahouse designed by Fumai: the Kanden-an (Figs. 134, 164). The central post in the tearoom rises from a central floorboard about 1.4 *shaku* (about 42 centimeters) in width. Deviating from the customary usage, which placed the hearth next to the central post—the so-called *daime* arrangement—this room has a corner hearth. The central post was placed so as to support the shelf, and the floorboard was inserted to create a feeling of spaciousness. Here, too, can be seen Fumai's freedom in devising the structure. Yet the Fumai who emerges here as a man breaking through current molds and advancing the cause of unconventional modes of expression in no way rushed along arbitrarily and never ceased to tread

166. Interior view of San'un no Toko tearoom. 1800. Koho-an, Daitoku-ji, Kyoto.

squarely within the framework laid down by the rules of tea.

The basis for Fumai's freedom of expression in teahouse design lay in the works of classicism. The Yugetsu-ken teahouse of the Osaki-en was clearly inspired by the Konnichi-an, the Kan'un teahouse (Fig. 165) by the Tai-an, and the Shoka teahouse by the Shoka-do. Of the Kan'un teahouse, the *Osaki-en Ki* (Records of the Osaki-en) says that "among Lord Fumai's choices, only this teahouse gave him complete satisfaction." Fumai, who in his *Matsudaira Fumai Cha-no-yu Kokoroe* (Matsudaira Fumai's Notes on the Tea Ceremony) states that "we should take advantage of the works of outstanding predecessors no matter what their school," assimilated the outstanding works of classicism and showed that his attitude was to let them reflect for

him the "changing phases of the years." He molded his style after that of Enshu, in whose school he had taken his first lessons in tea; lent his efforts to the reconstruction of the Koho-an, gutted by fire in 1793; and, behind the Jikinyu-ken of the Daitoku-ji, built a copy of the Mittan tearoom of the Ryoko-in. Yet here again his creative impulse sought, by means of delicate artifices of design, to satisfy the feelings of a new age, taking care all the while not to mar the dignity of the original work.

Fumai was not a tea master but simply a *sukisha*, a lover of tea. His earnestness in studying classical teahouses would later exert a strong influence on other *sukisha*. It may be said that the respect for classicism and the fashion of copying that characterized the Meiji (1868–1912) and Taisho (1912–

167. *Tea bowl called Kaga, formerly owned by Matsudaira Fumai. O-ido ware; diameter, 15.2 cm. Fifteenth or sixteenth century.*

168. *High-shouldered tea caddy called Aburaya Katatsuki, formerly owned by Matsudaira Fumai.*

1926) eras owed their beginnings to the commendable achievements of Fumai.

THE YEARNING FOR MEIBUTSU It was Juko who had "no taste for the full moon" and responded instead to the bare simplicity of the Ise and Bizen wares. But this is not to say that he had no attachment to famous wares. On the contrary, and thanks to his abundant wealth, he was known in his day precisely as a leading collector of such wares. The same could be said of Takeno Jo-o, to say nothing of Rikyu, who, while laying down the principle that "the *cha-no-yu* consists merely of heating water and serving a cup of tea," was at the same time collecting famous utensils. Even those men who displayed a deep feeling for the *wabi* style were overcome with a strong yearning for renowned wares. The taste of each succeeding generation, beginning in a sense with the Ashikaga shoguns Yoshimitsu and Yoshimasa, was to reflect the desire for these wares,

harbored in the hearts of tea men as well. Among those who sought them were some, such as Oda Nobunaga and Toyotomi Hideyoshi, who craved possessions as a means of displaying their power, but in the case of most men the yearning for such wares was motivated simply by a deep attraction to the beauty, quality, and taste they found in them. Since entertainment was an essential element of the *cha-no-yu*, it was only natural for men to acquire a taste for collecting *meibutsu*. In fact, the absence of that taste in Koetsu and Sotan was the exception rather than the general rule.

The infatuation with renowned wares is illustrated in a story dealing with one of the three most famous Ido bowls: the Kizaemon Ido (Fig. 141), a sixteenth-century Korean masterpiece presently owned by the Koho-an at the Daitoku-ji. Around the end of the seventeenth century, a rich Osaka merchant named Takeda Kizaemon treasured with great affection this tea bowl of the O-ido type. In time, however, he lost his wealth and was

169. Returning Sails on a Vast Bay, *attributed to Mu-ch'i (Fa-ch'ang), formerly owned by Matsudaira Fumai. One of a set of eight hand scrolls entitled* Eight Views of the Hsiao and the Hsiang. *Southern Sung dynasty, thirteenth century.*

reduced to the condition of a beggar. Despite having to part with everything else, he could never bring himself to give up the O-ido tea bowl, and finally, agonized by the sores that covered his entire body, he died embracing the bowl. From this event there developed a legend to the effect that all subsequent owners of the bowl—targets, perhaps, of Kizaemon's revengeful spirit—would be stricken with sores. Indeed, Matsudaira Fumai and his son Gettan, who in turn became later owners of the bowl, were afflicted as foretold in the legend. After Fumai's death, his wife presented the bowl as a gift to the Koho-an, the site of Fumai's tomb, so that prayers could be said for the repose of Kizaemon's soul. There is no doubt that being charmed by tea bowls to the point of excess has led to strange happenings in every age, and there are stories similar to this one connected with many of the famous tea utensils.

We have already noted that *meibutsu,* in the broad sense of the term, are of three classifications: *o-meibutsu, meibutsu,* and *chuko meibutsu.* Let us review these classifications here. *O-meibutsu* are those considered as famous wares before Rikyu's time and include the Higashiyama *gomotsu,* or tea utensils stored in the family repositories of the Ashikaga shoguns. *Meibutsu,* in its narrower sense, denotes those famous wares newly evaluated as such in the days of Rikyu and Oribe, while *chuko meibutsu* are those subsequently added in Enshu's time. This system of classification dates back to the days of Enshu. With the establishment of the Tokugawa government, under which the daimyo of each fief ruled his own domain, the ambition of many daimyo to make a display of their authority led them naturally to seek possession of famous wares. Enshu produced *meibutsu* and drew up a system of classification—an undertaking that can be viewed as a response to the demands of his time. And the daimyo and wealthy merchants sought, by adding at least one more variety of *meibutsu* to their collec-

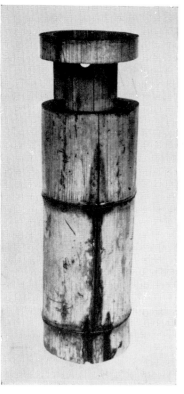

170. One-tiered bamboo flower container called Onjo-ji, by Sen no Rikyu, formerly owned by Matsudaira Fumai. Sixteenth century. Tokyo National Museum.

tions, to draw attention to their refined taste. In this sense, what is popularly known today as the "tea of utensils"—that style in which the utensils are placed on display—may be said to have flourished from the time of Kobori Enshu.

The early Edo period saw the publication of two books that were a clear expression of the current rage for *meibutsu*. They were the *Matsuya Meibutsu Shu* (Collection of Matsuya's Renowned Wares) and the *Ganka Meibutsu Ki* (Catalogue of Renowned Objects of Pleasure), of which the former concerned the collection of *meibutsu* owned by Matsuya Hisamasa (?–1598). That the exaltation of *meibutsu* in subsequent times dates from the days of Enshu is clear if we consider that the *Ganka Meibutsu Ki* was printed in 1660, not too many years after Enshu's death in 1647.

The *Ganka Meibutsu Ki*, by an unknown author, lists the possessions of the Tokugawa shoguns and other notables. It was compiled in the course of a reassessment, from the viewpoint of Enshu's day, of the *meibutsu* from the Higashiyama period up to the time of Rikyu and Oribe, and it contains hardly a mention of *meibutsu* newly fancied during the period when Enshu flourished. About thirty years later, however, there appeared another work, the *Chuko Meibutsu Ki* (Record of Rediscovered Renowned Wares), which made frequent reference to Enshu's age and particularly to the *Enshu Kura Cho* (Records of Enshu's Storehouse). At this stage a considerable change is apparent in the items designated as *meibutsu*. Of the Chinese paintings, mention is made of no more than two or three, among them the *Persimmons* and *Chestnuts* attributed to Mu-

171. Kofuki *(powdery) tea bowl, formerly owned by Matsudaira Fumai. Diameter, 14.8 cm. Yi dynasty, fifteenth or sixteenth century. Hatakeyama Museum, Tokyo.*

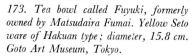

173. *Tea bowl called Fuyuki, formerly owned by Matsudaira Fumai. Yellow Seto ware of Hakuan type; diameter, 15.8 cm. Goto Art Museum, Tokyo.*

172. *Tea bowl called Miyamaji (Mountain Path), formerly owned by Matsudaira Fumai. Okugorai Karatsu ware; diameter, 14.1 cm. Early seventeenth century.*

ch'i and now stored in the Ryoko-in subtemple of the Daitoku-ji. The scrolls consist largely of examples of calligraphy, including poems inscribed by Teika. Other than these, the outstanding items are an example of calligraphy by Seigan Soi (1588–1661), abbot of the Daitoku-ji and friend of Hosokawa Sansai; the death poems of Rikyu and Sotan; tea bowls by Koetsu; and numerous works of the early Edo period.

THE UNSHU MEIBUTSU

The collecting of *meibutsu* continued in vogue through most of the eighteenth century, during which time it brought about the appearance of a great and unique collector, Matsudaira Fumai, whose career in the world of tea we have already noted.

Among the outstanding collectors of tea utensils during the Edo period there were, apart from the shoguns, such daimyo as Maeda Toshitsune, third-generation lord of the Maeda fief in Kaga Province; Inaba Masamichi, titular governor of Mino Province; and Tsuchiya Masanao, titular governor of Sagami Province. To these must be added the daimyo connected with the shogunate cabinet, who were also the owners of large collections. Yet none of them were in the class of the titular governor of Izumo, Matsudaira Harusato, namely Fumai, whose collection was on a scale unexampled before his time. Rated one of the top *cha-no-yu* men in his day, he also wrote the earlier noted eighteen-volume work *Classified Collection of Renowned Wares of Ancient and Modern Times,* popularly referred to as the "Book of Eighteen Volumes." But it was his vast collection of famous utensils, known as the

174. Top: tea bowl called Ojio, formerly owned by Matsudaira Fumai. Ko-ido ware; diameter, 14.7 cm. Sixteenth century. Bottom: lids of boxes for the tea bowl.

Unshu Meibutsu, or renowned wares of Unshu (Izumo Province), that served more than anything else to bring his name into the limelight.

The Unshu Meibutsu comprised a total of 583 tea utensils. On the strength of his own connoisseurship Fumai classified these in five major categories, which he headed "treasures," "*o-meibutsu*," "*chuko meibutsu*," "general *meibutsu*," and "high-class *meibutsu*." Listed in the "treasures" section are pieces that he considered outstanding among the *o-meibutsu,* and here we have evidence that gives us an insight into the depth of Fumai's vision. The entire collection cost him the colossal sum of 85,745 *ryo,* or 464 coins of gold, plus gold weighing 170 kilograms, and 3,900 coins of silver, plus silver weighing 65 kilograms. He had a box made for nearly every famous object in his collection, and on the box, which itself was of the highest-quality material, he himself inscribed the *hakogaki* in his peculiar style, borrowed heavily from that of the Teika school (Fig. 174). Even the box-wrapping cord, the paper to safeguard the box from soiling, and the overall cloth cover, he had made to suit his own taste. When Fumai made his journeys to and from Edo for the alternate-year residence (*sankin kotai*)—a measure of control enforced by the shogunate on the daimyo—his servants invariably bore with them three famous treasures: the Aburaya Katatsuki, a high-shouldered tea caddy (Fig. 168); the Yari no Saya (Spear Sheath), another high-shouldered tea caddy (Fig. 39); and the calligraphic work called the *Nagare Engo* (Fig. 136), an authorization for the teaching of Zen written by the Chinese monk Yuan-wu K'o-ch'in (in Japanese, Engo Kokin) for one of his disciples. From this fact alone we can judge the greatness of Fumai's affection for his tea-ceremony objects. And yet we see another aspect of him in his conduct at tea parties. Despite his possession of such a vast collection of tea utensils, he invariably arranged only those that truly suited his own taste and never once organized a party for the sake of displaying his wealth.

An interesting characteristic of Fumai's collection is that nearly all the works included in it were bought through dealers in tea utensils. In fact it is from the time of Fumai that this new role of the utensil dealer as purchasing agent is thought to have developed. In this way, too, his collection can be said to have made a mark on its age. But Fumai's fancy for collecting *meibutsu* was one that only a rich daimyo could have afforded.

CHAPTER SEVEN

Tea as a Work of Art

FROM THE OPENING of the country in 1853 through the Meiji Restoration (1868) and beyond, Japan was swept by a surging wave of Westernization—the wave of "civilization and enlightenment," as it was called. The tea cult, nurtured as in a hothouse throughout feudal society, felt the impact quite early and moved into a period of crucial change. By that time the tea men connected with the shogunate, as well as tea-loving daimyo, had already been deprived of their stipends; the tea masters of various schools were obliged to obtain licenses as instructors in the entertainment arts; and famous utensils owned by the tea masters and many former fief lords were classified and placed on the market.

It was during these years that Gengensai Soshitsu (1810–77), ninth-generation grand master of the Ura Senke school, proved himself a worthy son of the Restoration. At an exhibition held in Tokyo in 1873 he introduced the use of chairs in the tea ceremony in deference to those guests who attended in Western clothes. It was also he who, foreseeing that increasing travel would lead to an increase of people on the road, devised a portable tea set enclosed in a small box for use during leisure hours at inns. Viewed from a present-day perspective, the tea ceremony with chairs can be seen to have its roots far back in the tea practices of the Heian court, but in the days of Gengensai it was looked on as a novelty. A response such as this to the demands of the changing times did not always meet with the approval of the tea world and often took shape in the midst of violent criticism and disdain, even though backed by a sure insight into future trends. Gengensai, as the eldest among the hereditary grand masters of the Sen family, provided chado with a period of brilliant leadership that enabled it to weather times of severe distress.

The trend of "civilization and enlightenment" gradually came to fuse with hopes for a revision of the unequal treaties that the Tokugawa shogunate had concluded with Western powers after 1854 and constituted the first step in the ascent to the highest level of Europeanism. The peak was attained in 1883 with the construction of the Rokumeikan hall, where glittering high-society balls were conducted in the same style as the ones Westerners were known to enjoy. At the same time, however, there came a reaction to this outward-looking tendency in the form of a new and careful look at Japan's traditional culture. This in turn engendered a clamor for the preservation of national characteristics. Standards of the Noh and the Kabuki were improved. Japanese fine arts benefited from a reassessment by Ernest Fenollosa (1853–1908), an American researcher of Japanese art and one of the founders of the Tokyo Art School (present Tokyo University of Arts), and others. The new trend was accelerated by the opinions voiced by men like the critic Miyake Setsurei (1860–1945), a frequent contributor of

175. *Tea-ceremony arrangement with chairs in Mujaku-ken tearoom. Devised in 1873. Horinouchi family, Kyoto.*

his nationalistic views to the magazine *Nihon Oyobi Nihonjin* (Japan and the Japanese). As the movement grew, it also affected the world of tea, which at the time likewise stood poised for a new start. The *iemoto* system, too, once on the verge of dissolution, was then reorganized.

TENSHIN AND "THE BOOK OF TEA" Okakura Tenshin (or Kakuzo; 1862–1913) was born the son of a Yokohama trader. On graduating from the Tokyo Imperial University he entered the Ministry of Education and soon joined forces with Fenollosa to pursue the rediscovery of beauty in Japan. Appointed a member of the Arts Investigation Committee, he was then delegated to go to Europe in the company of the committee chairman, Hamao Arata (1849–1925), and from that distance he saw the art of his homeland in a new light.

Japan became involved in wars with China from 1894 to 1895 and with Russia from 1904 to 1905 and subsequently made rapid strides in the direction of capitalism. In October 1902, when Tenshin was again in Europe, he published in London *The Ideals of the East*. In time he was named adviser to the Boston Museum of Fine Arts. While in New York, in 1904, he wrote *The Awakening of Japan* and in 1906 *The Book of Tea*. Through the medium of these books, all of which were written in English, he contributed greatly to introducing Japan's cultural tradition overseas. Yet these were by no means merely propagandistic writings. When in April 1927 the Japanese version of *The Book of Tea* made its first appearance, the spirit of tea described in its pages caused deep stirrings in the minds of the Japanese people and aroused them to a new understanding of the tea ceremony, looked upon at the time as no more than

176. Tearoom, *by Yasuda Yukihiko.*

and now the newly emerging wealthy class began to direct its attention toward tea as a means of social advancement. It was the members of this class who became the leaders in the new taste for *meibutsu* and sought to collect the famous wares released by the former daimyo and the declining upper class of the time. They were typified by the Iwasaki family, which made its fortune in the Mitsubishi Steamship Company. In 1876 Iwasaki Yanosuke acquired the Tsukumo Nasu tea caddy, an *o-meibutsu.* Subsequently the Mitsui, Konoike, Sumitomo, and other wealthy families whose prosperity dated back to the Edo period consolidated their status as zaibatsu and took an active interest in the collection of renowned utensils. Typical of this group in the early years of the present century were Fujita Denzaburo, a businessman with political affiliations; Kano Jihei, who acquired fame in the business world as a brewer in Nada, Hyogo Prefecture; and Nezu Kaichiro, who won a name for himself as business director of the Tobu Railway Company and founded the Nezu Art Museum in Tokyo.

These three patrons of the arts shared a common feature. In order to preserve their collections intact, they established museums in which they could be displayed to the public. Their action deserves the highest appreciation, for it stressed the role of the tea cult in preserving cultural assets that are important elements of art in general. In this sense it can be said that the spirit of Tenshin's declaration was to a certain extent realized.

During the ensuing years, which stretched like a valley between the two world wars, men like Kobayashi Ichizo (also known by the art name Itsuo), founder of the Hankyu Electric Railway Company, and Matsunaga Yasuzaemon (also known by the art name Jian), president of the former Toho Electric Power Company, provided strong leadership in the world of tea. They, too, gave evidence of the deep understanding of art that had characterized their predecessors.

In the background of all this movement an organization known as the Daishikai—named after the priest Kobo Daishi (Kukai; 744–835), founder of the Shingon sect of Buddhism—was established

a polite accomplishment for people of means. Tenshin's statement in this book that "tea is a work of art and needs a master hand to bring out its noblest qualities" constitutes a strong affirmation of the artistic quality in tea. He was in all likelihood, too, the first to discuss tea as an art. And yet, in Okakura's view, the emphasis on tea as a way of Zen stands out in marked relief, and this also explains why the book became such a popular classic for use in teaching within the orthodox *iemoto* system. Again, in facing up to the fact that the tea ceremony was on the way to becoming just another entertainment, it also served as a warning to the public to re-examine its attitude carefully.

Paralleling the growth of a capitalistic society, the way of tea found new patrons among men of means. The very fact of their tradition gave to the old, rich families a solid grounding in the arts,

177. View of Rinshun-kaku, a villa in the sukiya *style. Originally built in 1649; relocated in 1915. Sankei-en, Yokohama.*

in 1895 by Masuda Takashi (art name, Don'o; 1848–1938), whose position at the time in the Mitsui firm was equivalent to that of a present-day general manager. The members of this organization, important leaders in financial circles centered in Tokyo, took turns in giving tea parties, access to which became a status symbol in such circles. At the core of this activity lay the tea ceremony, which thus came to signify a form of cultivation for business executives. Besides Masuda and Nezu, leading figures around whom the Daishikai attained ever increasing popularity were Fujiwara Ginjiro (1869–1960), prominent in the Mitsui zaibatsu and founder of the Oji Paper Company, and Hara Tomitaro. This trend was not entirely unrelated to the increase in the practice of the tea cult among women and as a club activity at places of work, especially in large companies. Correspond-

ing to the Tokyo-centered Daishikai in the Kanto region, the Juhachikai, or Society of Eighteen, emerged in the Kansai region, centered in Osaka. This group was dissolved at the time of the Russo-Japanese War, was then reorganized in 1915 under the name Koetsukai (Koetsu Society), and as such is still active today. These organizations became vehicles for the exhibition and appreciation of old art that comprised mainly tea utensils. They had a marked influence on dealers in old art at the time, and they contributed in no small way to the rise in the standard of appreciation shown by the general public.

In this way, the perception that "tea is a work of art" reached new depths. Yet the very fact that tea was now looked upon in this fashion brought on a new danger: that of yet another tea centered on utensils. As Tenshin himself stated in *The Book*

178. Tearoom in Sogo Department Store, designed by Murano Togo. About 1941. Osaka.

of Tea, "They want the costly, not the refined; the fashionable, not the beautiful." He had never meant to encourage such a line of thought, for his intention was to stress that tea is an art, not art objects.

THE ARTISTIC VALUE OF TEA We must not lose sight of the fact that tea, while supported by the spirit of Zen as emphasized by Tenshin, was originally an entertainment. As Rikyu himself implied in his statement that "the *cha-no-yu* consists merely of heating water, serving tea, and drinking it," it is easy to look on tea merely as an object of private interest. But in fact a social relationship in the form of tea gatherings already existed in the society where it was nurtured, and thus it was an entertainment supported strongly both by the individual and by society. In other words, the tearoom is a stage, and the program for the tea ceremony is the playscript in conformity with which the stage properties (tea utensils) are arranged. If, in addition to this, the host be considered the actor and producer, and the guests the audience, a tea party may then be compared to a one-scene stage art.

The keynote of this art is the *furyu* we have already touched upon. In olden times *furyu* meant "elegance" and "refinement" and later came to signify "amusement." Taken literally, however, it embraces the two concepts of tradition and creation, and it has its foundation in the classics. That being the case, the artistic quality of *chado*, insofar as *furyu* is at its core, is revealed when its harmony as a performance is established. Art in tea consists in the beauty displayed in the harmonious arrangement of various carefully selected utensils set down in the program for the tea ceremony. The process of artistic creation is truly nothing other than the occasion for the training of the intellect and the senses. *Chado* blends historical tradition with mod-

179. View of Miyuki Room in Hassho-kan restaurant, designed by Horiguchi Sutemi. 1950. Nagoya.

ern creativity, and thus the intellect and the senses of the people involved with it must be employed and cultivated to their utmost limit.

THE RE-CREATION OF HISTORICAL TEA PARTIES If one thinks along these lines, then not only is the art in tea something to be constantly created anew, but it is also possible, with the aid of complete tea records, to re-create historical tea parties of the past to the same extent that it is possible to re-create Noh and Kabuki performances. In fact, since it was one of the aims of this book to present this aspect of art in the tea ceremony, we undertook to re-create in imagination a number of tea parties at various points in history where outstanding actor-producers—that is, celebrated tea masters—made their appearance.

It is fortunate indeed that famous tea utensils can be admired and appreciated as they are pre-served today in the display cases of museums and art galleries, but it must be admitted that when they are viewed in this way they are nothing more than historical relics. We felt that if it were possible to place such objects in actual tea-party settings, they would for the first time regain their former life. As a first attempt, we obtained special permission to borrow the bamboo flower container Yonaga (Long Night), a highly treasured rare utensil now preserved in the Fujita Art Museum in Osaka, and to hang it in the tokonoma of the Tai-an tearoom at the Myoki-an. By placing it there, we succeeded in creating a totally fresh, as well as historical, tea atmosphere (Figs. 6, 180, 196). Again, wondering what might possibly once have been displayed on the "Sowa shelves" in Ichijo Ekan's villa, we went back to that moment in history and pondered all the likely ways in which the tearoom might have been decorated. The result was a room filled with a classical aroma

180. *Two-tiered bamboo flower container called Yonaga, by Sen no Rikyu.*

昭和二年三月八日㊞
菩碧重重 太郎㊞
主益 由銘翁

寄附
梶掲 江月筝平心文
時代蒔絵鶴亀小硯箱
長好 小色紙
自在竹手桁ヶ潜慶作銘露挂ヶ籠㊞
手取釜 楽長次郎作
登
蓋置 書砂中かゝ二本鈎書砂秘室

181. *Record of a tea party given on March 8, 1927, by Masuda Don'o. Masuda family, Tokyo.*

inconceivable until now (Figs. 102, 200). Seen in this light, the art in the tea ceremony does not acquire its meaning from the beauty of each of the parts but is best savored as a blending of all of its elements into a new synthesis.

Yet the story does not end there. What we succeeded in savoring in this revival of historical tea parties was the actual feeling that tea is indeed an art of hospitality. To organize a successful tea party and make the best possible arrangement of tea utensils requires a great deal of hard work. One must literally be on the go, or, as the saying has it, "run from east to west."

The word *chiso* in Japanese literally means "running around or busying oneself to prepare a good reception." Today, its honorific form, *gochiso*, has come to mean a banquet of delicious foods. The core of its meaning, however, when the term is used in expressing thanks to a host, is not to denote satisfaction over the delicacies themselves but rather to indicate a grateful acceptance of the treat painstakingly prepared by the host for his guest—that is, as an act of hospitality. This in turn explains the use of the honorific form to express the guest's feeling of appreciation. In the priests' living quarters of Zen temples in Kyoto, a statue of the swift-footed warrior deity Ida Ten (in Sanskrit, Skanda) is commonly worshiped. This warrior is said to run 3,000 *ri* (about 7,000 miles) in an instant, and his being thus honored is a symbol of the mental preparedness to take the trouble of providing the utmost hospitality. *Chiso* is certainly not a word that applies only to the meal accompanying the tea ceremony. Rather, the art in the tea ceremony itself demands the kind of hospitality born of such a spirit.

CHAPTER EIGHT

The Design of the Tea Garden and the Teahouse

WE DO NOT KNOW the size of the *yamazato*, or "mountain-village gardens," of the Nakarai Ro-an teahouse or of the teahouse in the Ishiyama Hongan-ji, head temple of the Shin sect of Buddhism in Osaka, both of the mid-sixteenth century. Nor do we know the size of the garden at Soju's Shimogyo teahouse of the early sixteenth century, of which it was said: "In the very heart of the city I have the impression of being in the country." It is certain, nevertheless, that the environmental make-up of the area surrounding these teahouses took its direction from what was known as the *yamazato*. We learn from the *Yamanoue Soji Densho* (Writings of Yamanoue Soji) that at Juko's teahouse there was "a large willow in the front courtyard and several pines visible beyond the garden wall" and that at Jo-o's there were "many large and small pines in the courtyard and beyond it."

THE COURTYARD AND THE ROJI Jo-o's 4.5-mat room (Fig. 21), as noted by Soji, was adjoined by a "front court-yard" and a "side courtyard." According to a drawing by Ikenaga Sosa, the former constituted the "garden" and the latter the "inner path." The "side courtyard" undoubtedly meant an approach leading up to the teahouse—in other words, a *roji* (alley, or garden path). Close to the entrance of the teahouse there must have stood a *chozubachi*, or high basin for the guests to wash their hands. The origin of the *roji* can be traced to the overcrowded living conditions in the towns (Fig. 192). As for the "front courtyard," it seems to have been created as a garden facing the veranda. Its width, according to the *Sekishu Daiku no Sho* (Sekishu's Carpentry Book), was "4.7 *shaku* [about 1.42 meters] from the veranda post to the earthen wall." Why was this enclosed garden adopted? The reason is that the teahouse depended for its illumination on the entrance opening out onto the veranda. And in the absence of benches in the garden at this early time, the view of a garden was needed so that the veranda could be used as a waiting place for guests during the *nakadachi*, or intermission in the tea ceremony, when the host prepared for the next part of the proceedings. At the same time, however, as explained in such early tea books as the previously noted *Senrin*, "the guests ought not to be distracted by the garden, so that they can devote themselves wholeheartedly to the *cha-no-yu* and

182. *Waiting bench of En-an teahouse. Originally built about 1640–55; rebuilt about 1867. Yabunouchi school of tea, Kyoto.*

183 (opposite page, left). *Bamboo* ▷ *fence in garden of En-an teahouse. Yabunouchi school of tea, Kyoto.*

184 (opposite page, right). *Cho-* ▷ *zubachi (high stone basin) in Ginkaku-ji style. 1486. Jisho-ji (Ginkaku-ji), Kyoto.*

to the appreciation of the *meibutsu*." To attain this end, the modes of expression used in the design of tea gardens at the time, such as "grass and trees, stones, sand, and gravel," had to be renounced absolutely. In their place, in order to "cool down the steam around the hearth and relieve the narrowness of the small tearoom," it was thought advisable to plant "grass and a few trees in the garden facing the anteroom or in the area of the basin." In this way, the composition of the teahouse and garden was completely unified in the pursuit of one sole aim, that of the *cha-no-yu*.

The use of a front and a side courtyard continued thereafter for a long time and was subsequently adopted in Rikyu's 3-plus-a-*daime*-mat tearoom in Osaka and again in a replica of the latter, the Sho-an tearoom. Yet there were times when these two courtyards were combined, as witness the teahouse built in 1587 in accordance with the plan prepared by Kusabeya Dosetsu (1573–1602), merchant and tea man of Sakai, on the grounds of Matsuya Hisayoshi's residence in Nara. This teahouse, according to the earlier noted *Cha-no-yu Hisho*, featured a straight stretch of *roji* surrounded on three sides by walls, one of which had a peep window looking out onto the street. Entrance to the *roji* was made from one of the sides, and from there steppingstones led up to the *nijiri-guchi*. Near the *nijiri-guchi* was a basin, and a single maple tree grew in the *roji* (Fig. 186). This side courtyard, preserving the appearance of the tea garden just as explained in older tea books, was a genuine *roji*—nothing more than an approach to the teahouse. The same can be said of the *roji* at the Tai-an. Here both the arrangement of flat embedded stones (*tatami ishi*) and smaller stones and the tall "sleeve-brushing pine tree" are new features, but insofar as it is a space composed by the very simplest means—just a *roji* and a basin —the garden shows no change. It is not clear when the stone path made its first appearance in the tea garden, but since, as Koshin states, Rikyu was inspired to use it after seeing the one at the Saiho-ji and introduced the *tatami ishi* for the first time when he built the Fushin-an at the gate of the Daitoku-ji, we could date it to 1584 or 1585. In the laying of these stones, several styles came into use. Doan placed them "for the sake of appearance"; Rikyu, "to give them a mellow look," we read in the *Hosokawa Sansai Ondenju no Sho* (Hosokawa Sansai's Book of Tea Rules). The school of

Rikyu "laid them by filling the space between the small stones with red and black earth," whereas Oribe's followers "cut them from Shirakawa stone [granite from Kita Shirakawa in Kyoto], making them 6 or 7 to 8 or 9 *shaku* [about 2 to 2.5 meters] in length and arranging small stones alongside them." This tradition, related in the *Chajin Keifu* (Genealogy of Tea Men), is well illustrated by the *roji* at the Tai-an and the En-an, which are representative of the two schools.

From about the middle of the Edo period, it became customary to set up the basin in combination with other functional stones: the front stone, the hot-water stone, and the lantern stone. In the *roji* at the Tai-an, in earlier days, a water basin called the Shibayama Chozubachi (named after its owner, Shibayama Kemmotsu) was used. This seems, according to Horiguchi Sutemi's *Rikyu no Chashitsu* (Rikyu's Teahouses), written in 1949, to have been a slightly shorter copy, made by Rikyu, of the "Ginkaku-ji style" basin (Fig. 184), square-shaped and with Genji incense symbols and lattice designs on the four sides, a product of Muromachi times. Tradition has it that Rikyu also made use of basins such as the Four-Sided Buddha, the Owl,

and the Big Round Stupa. Yet the one that most draws attention as being in the Rikyu style and is said by Sotan in his diary to have consisted of "a large natural stone hollowed out" is the basin at his Juraku residence. This basin is thought to correspond to the one that now stands in front of the Rikyu Memorial Hall at the Omote Senke school (Fig. 190). A small round hole has been carved in the upper surface to hold water. Here, in this natural-stone basin placed "as though creeping out of the ground," Rikyu's touch comes through to us most vividly.

FROM THE ROJI TO THE GARDEN In the *roji* of the above-described teahouse of Matsuya Hisayoshi there were no seating facilities, probably because there was a veranda at the entrance. By the time of Matsuya Hisayuki, in the mid-sixteenth century, there is said to have been "a 5-mat room in the *roji* for men to change into *hakama* [skirtlike trousers for formal use]." Later, at the 4.5-mat tearoom of Matsuya Kyuei, a tea bench made its appearance in the *roji*, and it was about this time, too, that a hanging sword rack came to be fixed to the outer wall of the

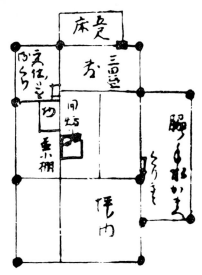

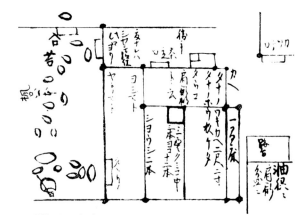

185. *Plan of Sen no Rikyu's 3-plus-a-daime-mat tearoom in Osaka, from* Yamanoue Soji Densho *(Writings of Yamanoue Soji).*

teahouse (Fig. 187). In any case, the veranda was finally removed from the entrance, its place taken by the bench, which thus came into general use. In other words, the loss of the function of the veranda led to the installation of facilities in the *roji*. The distance between the bench and the teahouse was required to be fairly short, since the bench served as a waiting booth both before the tea ceremony and during the *nakadachi*. There were, of course, limits to the size of the *roji* at any given teahouse; hence, if a considerable distance separated teahouse and bench, the *roji* had to be divided into the inner and the outer *roji*. To mark the boundary line between the two, a fence provided with a gate was erected, and on both sides of the fence a bench and a lavatory were installed. We have here, as it were, a drift toward the double- and triple-*roji* styles. Already in Rikyu's time, a structure akin to the double *roji* had taken shape in the garden of Hideyoshi's Hakozaki encampment in what is now Fukuoka Prefecture, and in all likelihood similar forms had also emerged in the several teahouses and *shoin* of Rikyu's Juraku residence. But it was Furuta Oribe who introduced the use of the double *roji* in full scale. In contrast with the narrowness

imposed on urban *roji* by the crowded residential areas, it was only natural for the *roji* of large daimyo mansions to expand in size. Tea parties were not limited to the *soan* tearoom but frequently combined the use of the *kusari no ma* and the *shoin*, and thus contact between the *roji* and the *shoin* garden became unavoidable.

In his own *roji*, Oribe freely adopted elements that Rikyu had been slow to use—for example, a stone lantern—and he also installed the "sleeve-brushing pine" (though not necessarily a pine) as a functional element and displayed, in addition, a penchant for showiness and elegance in his choice of the plants near the basin and of the stepping-stones near the bench. He also placed the bench for the nobility apart from the one for the other participants, as in the case of the En-an (Fig. 182). Evidenced in all the above creations and devices was the same brand of originality as marks his tearooms. Compared to earlier forms of expression that touched on the essence of the *roji* as just an access leading up to the teahouse, Oribe's *roji* contained abundant scenery and heralded the conversion of the *roji* into a garden. Through the mutual influence exercised by this style of *roji* and the *shoin*

186. Plan of Matsuya Hisayoshi's tearoom and garden, from Todai-ji version of Cha-no-yu Hisho *(Tea Ceremony Secrets). Built in 1587.*

187. Approach to Yu-in tearoom, showing hanging sword rack at upper right. Originally built about 1653; rebuilt in late eighteenth century. Ura Senke school of tea, Kyoto.

garden there emerged a new form of garden: the *chaniwa,* or tea garden, which, along with the development of the teahouse into the *sukiya* style of building, gradually took on the character of a spacious landscape. (It should be noted here that the word *roji* is still used as a synonym for *chaniwa.*)

The tea garden was not simply a yard. From the entrance onward, no ceiling or roof covered the garden, but it nevertheless formed with the teahouse an indivisible setting for the *cha-no-yu.* All the gates, beginning with the entrance to the tea garden, through the middle gate and middle wicket gate, up to and including the entrance to the teahouse itself, were to be "wriggled through." The basin was a *tsukubai,* which required users to crouch down. That is to say, both teahouse and tea garden were planned to maintain a low height—a space of low, flat structure.

THE FOUR-AND-A-HALF-MAT TEAROOM

Rikyu's Juraku residence included a 4.5-mat and a 2-mat tearoom. Though himself stressing that the true flavor of the *cha-no-yu* could best be found in the small *wabi* room, he nevertheless used the 4.5-mat

room more than any other throughout his lifetime. This room, too, went through a long process before its shape was perfected. From the earlier 4.5-mat rooms in Jo-o's style, said to have been located in his Sakai mansion and at the Shisei-bo subtemple of the Todai-ji, through the 4.5-mat room with an earth-floored area, constituting a transitional stage, there emerged at long last the definitive *soan*-style 4.5-mat room.

The 4.5-mat room said to have been built by Rikyu on the occasion of the Great Kitano Tea Party displayed a thorough *soan* technique. The roof was thatched, and the posts, including those that supported the eaves, were directly embedded in the ground—that is, with no foundation stones. In a word, it was an extremely simple structure. Two *shitaji mado* (lattice windows) and a skylight were the only sources of light for the guests' seats, which meant a very dim interior. However, a *bokuseki* (calligraphy) window was provided in the tokonoma. A similar *bokuseki* window could be seen in the 4.5-mat Rikyu tearoom handed down by Honkaku-bo, priest of the Mii-dera in Otsu, Shiga Prefecture, and a disciple of Rikyu's, but in the use of tokonoma windows Rikyu was generally conservative. The upper horizontal beam of the tokonoma frame was made from "a thick, round cryptomeria log cut square, with only the front surface left curved." The base of the frame was lightly lacquered, and the tokonoma ceiling stood at a most unusual height of 7.38 *shaku* (about 2.24 meters). The jambs of the *nijiri-guchi* consisted of logs with the bark attached, and the lintel on the side of the server's seat extended from wall to wall. By the utensil closet, too, there was a post. The corner post was "shaved from the floor up to a height of 2.5 *shaku* [about 76 centimeters], the shaved section being coated with plaster," according to the *Hosokawa Sansai Chasho* (Tea Book of Hosokawa Sansai). "Bark was attached at the point where the post emerged from the plaster," giving it a "distorted look." This method was known as the "toothpick post" or "plastered post" method. (See Foldout 1.)

Although in the 4.5-mat tearoom of Rikyu's Juraku residence there was only a slight shift in the location of the window for the guests' mats, there were numerous other and more significant changes. The *bokuseki* window was absent, as were also the post by the *nijiri-guchi*, the "toothpick post," and the lintel crossing the wall by the server's seat, with only the post by the utensil closet remaining. This tearoom can probably be considered to have been the consummation of the 4.5-mat room in Rikyu's own style. Sen Sotan built a 4.5-mat room in 1644 and another in 1653, and one of the two seems to have been a copy of the 4.5-mat room in Rikyu's Juraku residence. Most of the tearooms said to have been built in Rikyu's style during the Edo period in fact bore the marks of Sotan. The rules laid down by Rikyu concerning the location of the windows, the height of the ceiling, and so forth were observed in Sotan's 4.5-mat room, but the utensil-closet post finally disappeared, and the "toothpick post" replaced the embedded corner pillar, resulting in a spacious wall surface by the server's seat. Rikyu's works show a deliberate intent to preserve the spatial balance of the room through a dynamic equilibrium. To attain this goal he determined which posts should be retained and which eliminated.

One post consistently maintained ever since the early period of the 4.5-mat room was the one by the utensil closet. By means of this post he endeavored to give firm stability to the server's seat, an important element within the tearoom. Sotan, on the other hand, preferred to fashion a spacious server's seat and accordingly removed this post, installing in its stead a new post in the wall by the *nijiri-guchi*. He also turned his attention to the effect obtained by building the spatial structure as one unit, without isolating any of the wall surfaces, and by doing so tried not to demolish the expression of "quiet tension" he had inherited from Rikyu. The fascination in the shaping of the tearoom lies in the fact that, while at first glance it may look plain and frail, it always maintains a tense spatial structure. We find keenly pursued in it a technical finesse in the use of wall and post that is characteristic of Japanese architecture. That the books of tearoom modules employ the method of showing the absolute dimensions of each part, drawing examples from actual teahouses, indicates that the tearoom lacks the simple rules of modules employed for Shinto shrines, Buddhist temples, or palaces of the nobility, but it cannot be denied that it possesses instead a higher-level, more strict order of architecture.

THE DAIME-GAMAE AND THE DOAN-GAKOI

Around 1582, at his mansion in Osaka, Rikyu built a 3-plus-a-*daime*-mat tearoom. Yamanoue Soji, in a drawing of this room that he handed down, called it a "long, narrow 3-mat room" (Fig. 185). With its 5-*shaku* tokonoma and square tokonoma post, it still retained a rather old-fashioned shape. The server's seat and hearth formed a *daime* arrangement. Since a hanging shelf was installed, the room probably had a central post as well. In time, Rikyu's son Shoan built a replica of this tearoom in the Sen residence in front of the Hompo-ji temple in Kyoto. According to Matsuya's surviving drawing, the wall extending from the central post ran all the way from floor to ceiling, with no space left open at the bottom. This was probably a reproduction of Rikyu's 3-plus-a-*daime*-mat room in

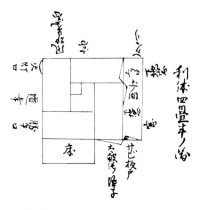

188. Plan of Sen no Rikyu's 4.5-mat tearoom with earth-floored area, from Izumi-gusa, by Fujimura Sogen.

189. Naka-kuguri (window-gate) in garden of Omote Senke school of tea, Kyoto.

Osaka. Hosokawa Sansai had a drawing that closely resembles Rikyu's 3-plus-a-*daime*-mat room, and he transmitted it as representing the origin of the *daime* style. What can almost certainly be considered the prototype of the *daime* arrangement in this tearoom is the positioning of the central post. In this kind of structure, the central post and the extended wall have the function of half isolating the server's seat from the guests' seats. In his *Sotan's Diary* Kamiya Sotan called this server's seat an "anteroom," a remarkably apt expression. Before the use of the term *daime* had become generalized, the server's seat in the *daime* style, set apart by the central post, was treated as another room. When we consider that the server's mat was placed in a far lower position than the guest mat in front of the tokonoma, as was the case in Rikyu's 3-plus-a-*daime*-mat room in Osaka, it becomes obvious that the server's seat was not for showing to the guests but intended rather to be kept modestly as an ante-room, and it was probably this idea that provided the inspiration for the *daime* style.

In the form known as the Doan-gakoi or Sotei-gakoi (so called after the merchant Sasaya Sotei of Sakai), a partition divided the server's seat from the guests' seats. The central post stood in the corner in front of the hearth, and from it stretched a wall with an arched doorway cut into it. This meant that the server's seat was visible only from the host's side of the central post. It was only when the host arrived with the utensils and opened the door that he came in contact with the guests' seats. There are various opinions as to whether the originator of this structure was Rikyu, Oribe, or Manase Dosan (1507–94), a doctor and an expert in *chado*, but nothing has finally been established. We may, however, affirm even more strongly than in the case of the *daime* setup that to convert the server's seat into an anteroom was an idea totally in keeping with the basic thinking of *wabi* tea, which

190. Tsukubai *(low stone basin)* in front of Rikyu Memorial Hall. About 1587. Omote Senke school of tea, Kyoto.

and a central post made of a crooked Japanese red pine. This style of room was continued in Sotan's Fushin-an, which was in time rebuilt in the 3-plus-a-*daime*-mat style, with the three mats laid parallel (*hira sanjo*). At any rate, the *daime* style based on the central post became the symbol of the *soan* tearoom. *Hosokawa Sansai's Book of Tea Rules* records that Rikyu wanted to install a central post in the 4.5-mat room but never carried his project through. This idea was developed by the samurai tea masters, beginning with Oribe, but insofar as they did it by simply adding a *daime* arrangement, they were probably not in line with Rikyu's original intention. Furthermore, the meaning of the *daime* style that reached the tearooms of Oribe and Enshu was exactly the reverse of its original conception, for in their rooms the arrangement was located where it would effectively provide a show for the guests. In the way of handling the Doan-gakoi enclosure, too, this trend was not entirely absent.

THE KOMA AND THE HIROMA
Tearooms are designated either as *koma* (small rooms) or as *hiroma* (large rooms), depending on whether they are smaller or larger than the 4.5-mat room. The option for use of the *daisu* in a 4.5-mat room allows the room to be used either as a *koma* or as a *hiroma*. Rikyu asserted that "the essence of the *cha-no-yu* is in the small room," and the idea that the tearoom had to be small became a dominant one. At the same time, however, the large room, or hall, also developed into an indispensable facility for tea parties. On such occasions the hall played the same role as the *shoin* (reception room), while it could also be used as a large tearoom, which in essence it was. And that is precisely the nature of Enshu's Bosen tearoom and others. Rikyu's Juraku residence had two such halls, which, in the diagram of the residence made in the Edo period, are labeled the Hiroma Dai Shoin and the Eighteen-Mat Colored Shoin. It is not far wrong to see them as corresponding to the hall and the *shoin* in samurai mansions of the time (Fig. 25).

The main body of the Hiroma Dai Shoin comprised an 18-mat room with a *nageshi* band of Japa-

was constantly fearful of allowing the server's seat to turn into an object of attraction for the guests. This effect was greatly emphasized in the late sixteenth and early seventeenth centuries by the introduction of the *mukogiri* style in the 3-mat room used by Sotan in the Sen family, mentioned in *Matsuya Kaiki,* and in the Yodomi no Seki tearoom of Fujimura Yoken (Fig. 145). The *mukogiri* was a style of cutting a place for the hearth in the server's mat at the end of the side faced by the host (server).

An important premise for the tearoom is that the server's seat should be in a lower position than the guests' seats, and in that sense these semi-isolating structures, whether the *daime-gamae* or the Doan-gakoi, served to mark out distinctly the position of the server's mat. A precedent for the separation of the room where tea was prepared from the one where it was served may be found in the "tea-boiling rooms" of the Ashikaga shoguns' palaces. When Rikyu first built a 1-plus-a-*daime*-mat room in Kyoto, he installed in it a *mukogiri*-style hearth nese cypress encircling the interior. The veranda was divided into two parts: the outer (or wider) and the inner. Half the width of the inner veranda was covered with mats bordering the threshold. The technique of combining a wide veranda with an interior one is useful when entry to the tearoom is made, in conformity with established tea manners, by edging forward on the knees. This suggests that it may have been devised by a tea man. Kamiya Sotan was invited by Rikyu to partake of *daisu* tea in this large room. The height of the ceiling was 10.4 *shaku* (about 3.15 meters); the roof was fitted with base rafters but no flying rafters; and the overall light appearance of the Hiroma Dai Shoin must have been reminiscent of that in the Manju-in temple in Kyoto, founded by Saicho around the turn of the ninth century. The Colored Shoin, on the other hand, employed the *menkawa* type of construction, in which the bark remained on the corners of the posts, and featured a 2-mat raised floor (*jodan*) and a 4-mat middle floor (*chudan*) with a *tsuke shoin*. It had no *nageshi*, and the ceiling was low—8 *shaku* (about 2.4 meters) in height—with a skylight opened in the open-timbered section over the *chudan*, giving it the repose of an unpretentious, low, flat tearoom. This room constituted the original model for the Zangetsu-tei and was used to welcome Toyotomi Hideyoshi on the occasion of his visit to Rikyu's residence. As *shoin*, the Hiroma Dai Shoin and the Colored Shoin were novel constructions. They followed the same construction principles as the tearoom—for example, the particularly low lintel (5.8 *shaku*, or about 1.76 meters, in the Hiroma)—and led to the birth of a new type of *shoin*.

Thus Rikyu, besides striving forcefully to perfect the spatial design for tea in the sphere of the *koma*, elaborately developed the architectural principles for the *hiroma*. His genius seems to have made itself felt in the structure of the entire Juraku residence, which was assessed by Sakuma Fukansai (1556–1631), a samurai who learned tea with Rikyu, as follows: "I find it hard to express in words how modest it is in contrast with the other houses there." When the design of the tearoom, condensed in the "small room," spread to the "large room"

191. *Steppingstone approach to Yu-in tearoom. About 1653. Ura Senke school of tea, Kyoto.*

and went on to affect the structure of the entire house, the *sukiya* style of construction made its appearance. This was an important landmark in the history of Japanese architecture, the consequence of the negation by tea architecture of the styles that had hitherto predominated. And it was indeed appropriate that the "first page" in the classic of *sukiya* architecture should have been illustrated by Rikyu's Juraku residence.

ORIGINALITY IN THE COMBINATION OF PARTS

The materials used in the teahouse cover a wide range. To mention only the logs, there were, besides those of natural wood with the bark attached, polished logs, patinated logs, spiral-patterned logs (created by binding young trees with rope), and others. In bamboo, too, the choice was wide. The variety of materials, all in their natural state, made for extreme diversification of texture and left little chance of dull uniformity. As a natural outcome,

193. Roji *of Omote Senke school of tea. About 1910–20. Kyoto.*

192. Roji *of Horinouchi residence. About 1869. Kyoto.*

not only the choice of each material but also their mutual combination emerged as an important problem. Depending on the combination, the room may lose its tranquility and lapse into loudness or coarseness, or it may become pretentious or, on the other hand, gentle. The concept underlying the design of the teahouse, as the book *Senrin* puts it, was that "it should neither contain strange styles nor draw attention." In developing, through the combination of several casual-looking parts, a fascination that attracted men powerfully to the tea world, Rikyu was indeed a genius. If these basics are departed from, a teahouse will not materialize, even if men's tastes change in time.

In the Bokaku-an tearoom at his Fushimi mansion, Oribe installed a central post of bamboo and was also known to make use of bamboo for underlining the *sodekabe,* the extended wall. It seems that Oribe liked the bamboo post, against which Rikyu

had cautioned, pointing out that "people without good connoisseurship use bamboo." He also used it for the jambs of the host's entrance. In the En-an style of teahouse, the host's entrance and the tokonoma are aligned. In such cases, Oribe maintained, according to the *Cha-no-yu Hisho,* that the base of the tokonoma frame should be lacquered black so as to harmonize with the bamboo jambs. If a round log were also used in the frame, it would mean too much "informal" material lining the same wall, with a consequent loss of dignity. While stressing the informal aspect by means of bamboo jambs, he did not fail to pay attention to the balance of the entire room and, to this end, added weight to the base of the tokonoma frame by lacquering it black. The tokonoma post, placed midway between the base of the tokonoma frame and the jambs of the host's entrance, had the corners broadly planed off and the surface roughly cut with an adze (Figs. 44,

45). Here we have a valuable example of the artist himself expressing his ideas about the combination of materials and, at the same time, a revelation of the sensitivity that Oribe brought to bear on the subject. And not only Oribe, but all the grand tea masters as well, produced such combinations in the display of their own particular tastes.

THE MODERNIZATION AND PRESERVATION OF TEA ARCHITECTURE

The search for ways to further the development of the teahouse after it had fallen into stereotyped forms was undertaken from early on, beginning with Matsudaira Fumai, and was more recently carried on by Sen Gengensai. Yet this problem still remains unresolved today. Early in the Meiji era, the Horinouchi family and Gengensai were quick to devise the tea ceremony with chairs (Fig. 175), and yet a new type of tearoom suitable for it was a long time in the making. A thorough plan for this new style of ceremony finally made its appearance after World War II at the New Japan Chado Exhibition, and in recent years facilities for it have also been installed by the tea schools, but a rough way still lies ahead before this type of room finds its perfect form. A new trend in the traditional tearoom saw the introduction of Western techniques, especially those used by modern architects in their construction of "new sukiya houses" built entirely by Western methods. This attempt resulted in an increase in the space of the tearoom, and a movement to modernize its design came to the fore. In such works the aim was to eliminate the use of timber wherever possible, beginning with the posts, and so to enlarge the wall surfaces. As a result, however, the appeal of the spatial tension, so strong in the classical tearoom, here became remarkably subdued. While the modernization of form continues to progress on its own, the essential content seems to be gradually losing contact with the spirit of tea. Modern teahouses require at least to be endowed with the fascination found in the spatial structure of the classical teahouse, and the principle of good combination of materials should continue to be pursued. Only then will the teahouse become united with the cha-no-yu within and the beauty of tea be fully developed.

We must remember, too, that it is in the stereotyped forms of the teahouse that refined architectural techniques nevertheless abide. In such teahouses, whose architecture displays a distinguishing characteristic in its use of natural logs, we can find traditions and nuances different from those found in such formal structures as Shinto shrines, Buddhist temples, and shoin. These traditions and nuances, for Japanese architecture, are a priceless inheritance whose history extends back further even than that of the teahouse itself. To effect the modernization of the teahouse naturally courts the collapse of traditional techniques. Therefore any effort made to promote new types of tearooms requires at the same time that these techniques not be forgotten.

CHAPTER NINE

The Beauty in Tea

FROM OLDEN TIMES, in the world of tea, many men of taste have concentrated their stock of knowledge on the creation of a comprehensive artistic environment, and theirs was not just a simple world in which one owned and appreciated a single scroll and a single tea bowl. To become a tea master was impossible without a deep foundation in the principles of tea. Without a delicate finesse of eye and heart and the feeling required to create a harmonious *ma,* or spatial relationship, the true value of the art in tea cannot be exhibited.

In that sense, Noami, Soami, Juko, Jo-o, Rikyu, Oribe, Enshu, Sowa, Sekishu, and Sotan were all undisputed masters in their day. It can be said that the styles of tea they displayed were reflected directly in the trends of aesthetic taste in their time. This chapter represents an effort to recollect the past from such a standpoint—that is, to recall the various tea styles through a re-creation of the atmosphere in which they were given expression.

THE BEAUTY OF WABI Symbolically presented in this section, beginning with Sen no Rikyu's tearoom where *wabi* tea took perfect shape, is the uniqueness of the beauty in tea as it is expressed in the Momoyama tea style, with its central concept that "any utensils may be used for the tea ceremony as long as their shape is good." As we look back at it from today, that beauty reveals a form derived from what Okakura Tenshin describes in *The Book of Tea* as "a worship of the imperfect." But clearly seen in its depths is the freedom of spirit and the strong volition that are so typical of the Momoyama age.

What is said to be the only extant architectural work of Rikyu is the tokonoma in the Tai-an tearoom. Here, with an arrangement of camellias in it, we hung one of his representative masterpieces: the Yonaga bamboo flower container (Figs. 6, 180, 196). There is no evidence that Rikyu himself ever made use of this arrangement, but the serene beauty that permeated the tokonoma when we placed the container there was absolutely startling. It had been some time since we first felt the urge to hang one of Rikyu's containers in this tokonoma, but the urge had been coupled with the apprehension that we might not succeed in creating a sense of *ma,* or spatial balance. Our fears were unfounded, however, and our apprehension gave way to a deep satisfaction when we were able to experience—true to life, as it were—one facet of Rikyu's taste. And this beauty surely embodies fully what he called the "break away from the world."

In seeking tea bowls of Rikyu's age one naturally turns to the O-ido and Chojiro bowls. And among the O-ido bowls, the most stylish is undoubtedly the one called Tsutsuizutsu (Fig. 7), owned at the time by Toyotomi Hideyoshi. Its unsophisticated but richly impressive shape represents the beauty of the "break away from the world," the beauty that stands in total contrast to the rounded beauty found in the art of the Sung and Yuan dynasties. The

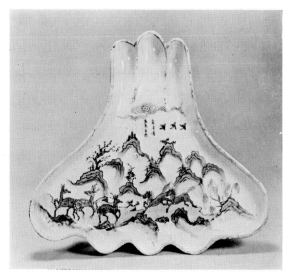

194. *Shallow bowl shaped like Mount Fuji, with design of deer and horses. Old Sometsuke ware; widest dimension, 28.4 cm. Ming dynasty, seventeenth century.*

beauty experienced here is indeed inexpressible in words.

The same feeling as aroused by the beauty of the Ido tea bowls is next evoked by the Chojiro tea bowls. The Ido bowl symbolizes the beauty of the uncontrived, but the Chojiro bowl in "Soeki's shape" is an achievement of the uncontrived after exhaustive trials in the contrived. Seated in the Tai-an with the Yonaga flower container hung in the alcove, one is tempted by a desire to hold in his hands Chojiro's Oguro bowl (Fig. 52) or else the Muichibutsu (Fig. 8). The wish goes unfulfilled, but one definitely senses that the unconcerned and balanced shape of the Muichibutsu would harmonize better than any other with the atmosphere in the Tai-an. At this point, too, one is sure to feel anew that the tea enjoyed by Rikyu in his late years was not the one that centered on the arrangement of famous utensils and that he preferred rather to create an aesthetic environment in keeping with the "break away from the world," the fruit of his own ideas.

Oribe's modeling symbolizes quite frankly a more "modern" consciousness of beauty. As a tea style of the Momoyama period it shows a deep penetration into creative artifice, the lack of which in Rikyu provides a strong contrast. That these two men appeared successively on the Momoyama scene is a vivid reminder of the extraordinary quality of that age.

Oribe's legacy is well illustrated by the En-an teahouse of the Yabunouchi school of tea in Kyoto (Figs. 10, 44, 45). Evident everywhere in it is the variegated creative artifice so typical of him, yet the overall simplicity remains intact. The greatest contrast, however, is in the tea garden. Rikyu sought above all to imbue the tea garden with an air of stillness. At Oribe's En-an, on the other hand, one has the strong feeling that he tried to create in the narrow garden as much breathing space as possible (Fig. 10).

With regard to tea utensils, the one that best illustrates Oribe's feeling, as does the Muichibutsu tea bowl in Rikyu's case, is the Iga flower container shown in Figure 9. It is of a bulky, unyielding character, and the creative artifice of the design, expressive of Oribe's strong self-assertion, effectively symbolizes his aesthetic consciousness. In the rough olive-brown surface of the container, reminiscent of some moss-covered boulder, we sense the disposition of the warrior. There is an intensity here, together with a feeling of reality, that we do not see in Rikyu's tea style, and we find it most persuasive.

Enshu lived neither the life of a merchant at the time when war ravaged the country in the late Muromachi period nor that of a warrior. His was, rather, the life of an extremely able construction-and-repair administrator. Accordingly, all through his tea style can be seen the effort to create a wide variety of tea situations through the use of all manner of utensils. Moreover, since this activity coincided with his holding the position of tea instructor to the shogun's household toward the middle of the seventeenth century, when the shogun's authority was taking firm hold, he naturally gave his closest attention to matters of style.

Enshu's taste is forthrightly shown in the Mittan tearoom (Fig. 11) in the Ryoko-in and the Bosen tearoom (Fig. 71) in the Koho-an, both located in the grounds of the Daitoku-ji temple. In the Mittan tearoom a clearly defined theme forms the core of the entire structure. It is a tearoom in a Zen temple, and it serves to display the calligraphic works of the abbot Mittan. Such an attitude toward tearoom design was to be found neither in Rikyu nor in Oribe, and in this kind of work Enshu's skill as an architect and as a producer of the tea ceremony was pre-eminent. The delicacy and richness of his ability in designing had never been within the reach of his two predecessors.

The tea style of the Momoyama period, for which "any utensils may be used . . . as long as their shape is good," gave birth around the 1570s or 1580s to a new form as seen in the Chojiro tea bowls of Rikyu's taste. Following this, between 1596 and 1614, Oribe's taste represented a further development in the free expression of the designer's will. The process continued into the mid-seventeenth century, which witnessed the rise of an absolutely superb artist in Koetsu and also the consequent development of a ceramic style instilled with a highly individual creative ingenuity that crystallized in remarkable shapes. Without doubt the Momoyama style of art, with its fondness for giving free expression to personal creativity, produced its brightest star in the

Raku ware that Koetsu molded with his own hands. In fact, he was the first really original artist to make a tea bowl. The significance of this achievement can be appreciated even more fully if it is remembered that the figure who attained this beauty of the unorthodox was not a professional potter but a man living a secluded life of *furyu*.

Koetsu, speaking of his own pottery making, says in the *Hon'ami Gyojo Ki* that "in pottery I realize I am better than the venerable Shojo [Shokado Shojo], and yet I have no wish to make a name for myself. All I want is to seek out good earth in Takagamine and occasionally to make pottery, but I have not the slightest ambition to cut a figure for myself in the pottery world." Such was definitely his state of mind, for a look at his tea bowls will reveal that he indeed had confidence in his ability in pottery. Naturally, since he was no professional potter, he frequently asked Raku Kichizaemon (1535–1635), second-generation head of the Raku family, and Raku Yoshibei (Donyu; 1599–1656), third-generation head of the family, to help him with the glazing and baking of the vessels. Koetsu also sought the assistance of a potter named Taemon. His own chief interest, therefore, obviously lay in the shaping of the bowls. In the process of molding a tea bowl from a lump of clay, the boldness of his approach, coupled with the fine delicacy in each stroke of the spatula, fashioned a beauty so rich that not even Chojiro or the famous Donyu could match it.

The outstanding masterpiece among the tea bowls of Koetsu is the Fujisan (Figs. 12, 69). Its decorous form combines a grave air with fineness of character. Rather than being just a tea bowl, it emerges as a work of carving and modeling, and as such it is an object of great fascination. To this bowl Koetsu himself gave the name Fujisan. He was probably inspired to do so because the white glaze he had applied to the entire surface of the bowl, when fired in the kiln, was transformed to lead gray on the lower half, suggesting Mount Fuji topped with snow. In any case, it is more than likely that Koetsu gave it the name because he himself sensed he had created something that could never be repeated.

195. *Detail of tea bowl called Seppo (Snow-covered Peak), by Hon'ami Koetsu. Red Raku ware.*

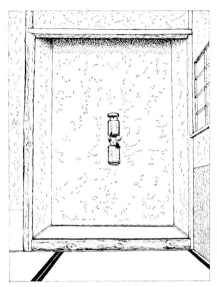

196. *Restoration of tearoom decoration in Sen no Rikyu's style: Yonaga flower container hung in tokonoma of Tai-an tearoom. (See also Figure 6.)*

The remaining bowls of outstanding merit held to be his authentic works total more than ten. The Red and Black Raku bowls each have a different air, and there are no two with the same feeling. In these bowls Koetsu pursued from various directions the possibilities of expressing the sense of beauty, and in this fact we find one of their most outstanding characteristics. Haiya Shoeki, in his *Nigiwai So*, tells us that after Koetsu's death people spoke with pleasure of his work as "interesting and possessed of character." Nor was that judgment limited to Shoeki's age, for even today high praise is lavished on his tea bowls, which are considered masterpieces of art in this genre.

Koetsu lived for the *furyu* of tea with a much greater intensity than either Rikyu or Oribe. As a pioneer in the way of tea too, he was in a position to provide his age with leadership and had, in fact, the real ability to do so. But he did not follow the same path as Rikyu, Oribe, and Enshu, who had been head tea masters and tea instructors to the shogun's household. As a member of the Hon'ami, a merchant family of Kyoto, he attended till the end to his family's business and, in addition, lived to his heart's content the life of a man of *furyu*. His career was truly a demonstration of the way of *suki*.

THE BEAUTY OF THE FORMAL, SEMIFORMAL, AND INFORMAL

In contrast with the foregoing section, which attempted to express symbolically the beauty of *wabi* tea, the present section will follow the stream that runs from the Higashiyama period, through Rikyu and Oribe, to Koetsu. With the help of two masterpieces of Sung and Yuan art, both highly esteemed during the Kitayama and Higashiyama periods, we can recall the *suki* for Chinese wares at the time. The *yohen temmoku* bowl shown here (Fig. 34) is of course the one referred to in the *Kundaikan Sa-u Choki* as follows: "This *yohen temmoku* is the best among the Chien bowls, though it is not very well known. It has a black ground covered with spots of light and dark lapis lazuli like stars. Mixed among these are touches of yellow, white, and very light lapis lazuli, and the glaze gives it a brocadelike effect. The price is incalculable." Today this masterpiece is famous the world over. Baked in the Chienyang kilns during the Southern Sung dynasty, it is known as the Inaba Temmoku because it was once in the possession of Inaba of Yodo in Osaka, the titular governor of Mino Province.

Mao Sung, painter of the *Monkey* (Fig. 33), is

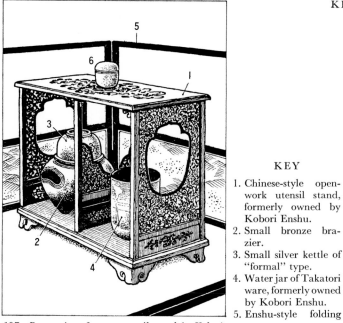

197. *Restoration of ornate utensil stand in Kobori Enshu's style: Kobori residence. (See also Figure 97.)*

made out in the *Nanso Inga Roku* (Catalogue of Southern Sung Academic Painting) to be the father of Mao I. His name also appears in the Tokugawa version of the *Kundaikan Sa-u Choki*, now in the possession of the Tokyo National Museum. The relevant entry there reads: "*Scenery of the Four Seasons: Flower, Bird, Monkey, and Deer* by Mao Sung."

This *Monkey* is, of course, attributed to Mao Sung and was formerly owned by Takeda Shingen (1521–73), lord of Kai Province (present Yamanashi Prefecture). In 1570, Shingen presented it to Kakujo, son of Emperor Gonara (1496–1557; r. 1526–57) and abbot of the Manju-in temple in Kyoto, where it has remained until the present day. Small in size, it possesses great dignity and is one of the outstanding examples of works transmitted from Sung and Yuan times.

The *haikatsugi* (ash glaze) *temmoku* tea bowl (Fig. 35) was handed down in the Tokugawa family of Kii Province (present Wakayama Prefecture). If, among the same Chinese *temmoku* bowls, those like the *yohen* and *yuteki* deserve to be characterized as having "formal" beauty, then this bowl clearly reflects the taste of the "semiformal." It is not very popular nowadays, but if we observe the harmonious air of *wabi* in the shape and the glaze, it becomes apparent that it represents a taste fully in keeping with that of the ages of Juko and Jo-o.

The *kofuki* tea bowl named Miyoshi (Fig. 36) was formerly owned by Miyoshi Chokei. It represents the stage of transition from the "semiformal" to the "informal"—that is, the years from the 1530s to the 1570s, when the taste for Koryo tea bowls was growing. It is conjectured that the earliest bowls to be introduced from Korea were those of Mishima and *kofuki* ware. As with the white *temmoku* tea bowl owned by Jo-o (Fig. 47), we can sense that the taste that found satisfaction in the texture of the white glaze was characteristic of an

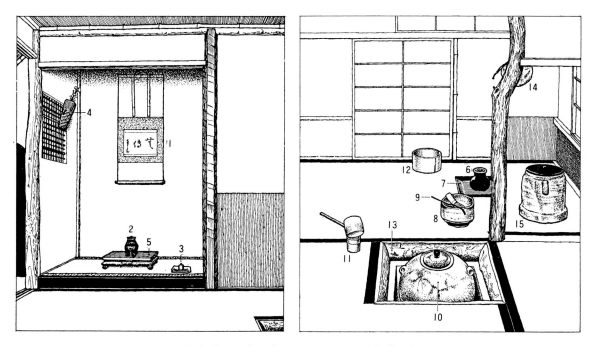

198. *Restoration of tearoom arrangement in Furuta
Oribe's style: En-an. (See also Figures 44, 45.)*

age that was, rather than completely informal, in a stage of transition from the semiformal to the informal.

The Old Seto tea caddy called Yari no Saya (Spear Sheath; Fig. 39) is a masterpiece regarded as the finest among Japanese tea caddies and was reportedly the possession of Toyotomi Hideyoshi. In the shape, with its air of having been copied from Chinese tea caddies, the robust creative originality that characterizes the Japanese pottery of Momoyama is lacking, and it is thought to have been baked in Seto during the late Muromachi period with heavy influence from Chinese wares.

The *daisu*, bronze utensil set, and Chojiro Black Raku tea bowl (named Kamuro) that adorn the Zangetsu-tei (Fig. 38), all transmitted as having been Rikyu's favorites, were in fact Rikyu's possessions and recall his *shoin* tea.

In the taste of the Momoyama daimyo for *meibutsu*, with Oda Nobunaga and Toyotomi Hideyoshi

as the central figures, the primary objective was to possess the set of paintings *Eight Views of the Hsiao and the Hsiang* by Mu-ch'i, the set of the same name by Yu-chien, and likewise the powdered-tea caddies and tea-leaf jars from the Eastern Hills Villa. The powerful men of the age, including Matsunaga Hisahide (1510–17; retainer of Miyoshi Chokei), Oda Nobunaga, Toyotomi Hideyoshi, and Tokugawa Ieyasu, did not fail to own, at one time or another, some of the *Eight Views*.

Mu-ch'i's large scroll *Returning Sails on a Vast Bay* (Fig. 169) was transmitted from Juko to Nobunaga and then to Kamiya Sotan and to Tokugawa Ieyasu. His *Evening Glow over a Fishing Village* (Fig. 31) was owned by Ieyasu and next by his tenth son, Tokugawa Yorinobu (1602–71). The *Wild Geese Descending over a Sandy Plain* went through the hands of Hideyoshi, his follower Uesugi Kagekatsu (1555–1623), and Uesugi Hidetada. The *Temple Bell in the Evening Mist* (Fig. 42) was in the posses-

KEY

1. Landscape ink painting by Soami hung in tokonoma. Inscription by the abbot Shumpo.
2. Bronze flower container called Hitosusuri. *Gomotsu* of Eastern Hills Villa.
3. Stand for flower container, formerly owned by Sen no Rikyu.
4. Inkstone case. Gold-lacquered design on cypress.

5. Movable black-lacquered utensil stand, formerly owned by Sen no Rikyu.
6. Kettle with double flange, by Tsuji Yojiro.
7. Bronze brazier designed for use on utensil stand.
8. Water jar, one of a set of bronze utensils formerly owned by Sen no Rikyu.
9. Ladle stand, one of a set of bronze utensils formerly owned by Sen no Rikyu.
10. Iron *hibashi* (charcoal tongs) with "happy old man" heads, formerly owned by Sen no Rikyu.
11. Waste-water jar, one of a set of bronze utensils formerly owned by Sen no Rikyu.
12. Tea caddy. Old Seto ware.
13. Tea bowl called Kamuro, by Tanaka Chojiro. Black Raku ware.
14. Tea scoop by Sen no Rikyu.
15. Lacquer tea caddy of type preferred by Takeno Jo-o.

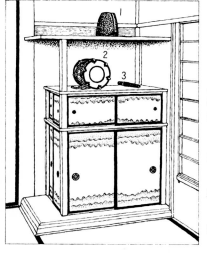

200. *Restoration of tearoom decoration in Kanamori Sowa's style: Ichijo Ekan's Nishikamo Villa tearoom. (See also Figures 100, 102.)*

KEY

1. *Kammuri* (old-time nobleman's formal headgear). Tsurugaoka Hachiman Shrine, Kanagawa Prefecture.
2. Hand drum, black-lacquered with gold-lacquered design of a floating chrysanthemum, by Mekura Orii. Konishi family, Kanagawa Prefecture.
3. Unsigned flute. Konishi family, Kanagawa Prefecture.

sion of Matsunaga Hisahide, Inaba Ittetsu (1515–88; samurai and follower of Nobunaga and Hideyoshi), Ieyasu, and Yorinobu.

Among the Chinese eggplant-shaped tea caddies, the Fuji Nasu (Fig. 41) is a highly prized masterpiece and constitutes, along with the Kokushi Nasu, a most remarkable pair. Owned by Oda Nobunaga, it later came into the possession of Maeda Toshiie and has remained until the present day in the collection of the Maeda family in Kaga, Ishikawa Prefecture.

The liking for calligraphy by Zen monks began with Juko and reached the peak of its popularity during the Momoyama period. Among Chinese works of calligraphy, the best are considered to be those of Yuan-wu (Fig. 136), while among Japanese works those of Daito Kokushi (or Shuho Myocho; 1282–1337), who founded the Daitoku-ji temple in 1324, are rated the best. The large two-character scroll known as *Plum Valley* (Fig. 40) was donated by the Zen priest Ikkyu to the Shuon-an, popularly known as the Ikkyu-ji temple, in Kyoto, where he spent his late years as a hermit. The third-generation lord of the Maeda fief of Kaga, Toshitsune, coveted it and eventually acquired it. It is said to be the best of Daito's outstanding calligraphic works.

Rikyu also preferred a calligraphy scroll in the tokonoma and often used a work by Liao-an Ch'ing-yu (Fig. 53). On such occasions he also often used the square kettle by Tsuji Yojiro (Fig. 43), one of his favorites, along with Chojiro tea bowls. Yojiro was the maker of Rikyu's kettles and was considered the best in his field in Kyoto.

The tea utensils we used in the En-an for our re-creation of a tea-party setting there were all either the original possessions of Oribe or those expressing his style. By means of the utensils with historical significance handed down in the Yabunouchi family of Kyoto, the owners of this teahouse, we were able to achieve a vivid revival of Oribe's tea here (Figs. 44, 45). The Shino water jar (Fig. 46) is a piece of Mino tea pottery that also represents Oribe's taste. The strong workmanship and the typical Shino tints of red in the gray glaze give it a beauty all its own.

The Goshomaru tea bowl called Furuta Korai (Fig. 63) is a Koryo bowl of the type said to have been made at the Kumhae kilns, near Pusan, Korea, after Hideyoshi's Korean campaigns and is said to have been designed on the basis of paper models that Oribe himself supplied. It is representative of the Koryo tea bowls favored by Japanese tea men.

The *Waka Makimono* calligraphy by Koetsu (Figs. 65, 88) and the tea bowls Seppo (Snow-covered Peak; Figs. 66, 195), Otogoze (Fig. 67), Shigure (Autumn Rain; Fig. 68), and Fujisan (Fig. 12, 69) conjure up vividly the life of *furyu* led by Koetsu at Takagamine. These four tea bowls in particular give a complete picture of his style.

THE BEAUTY OF REFINED RUSTICITY Works of art that reflect the tastes of Enshu, Sowa, and Yoraku-in, among the daimyo tea men, and Konoike Do-oku, Korin, and Kenzan, among the commoners, are presented here to show the beauty in tea during the century or so between the beginning of the Edo period in 1603 and the close of the Kyoho era in 1716.

The tea caddy called Osaka Marutsubo (Fig. 94) is reputed the best among the Seto tea caddies owned by Enshu, and in the *Collection of Matsuya's Renowned Wares*, too, it is recorded at the top of the list of Enshu's tea caddies. Enshu liked using the poetry of olden times as a source for the names of his utensils, and in the case of this *marutsubo*, or round jar, he associated its special character with the feeling in an old poem from the *Kokin-shu* that goes as follows: "In Osaka / the stormy wind is cold, / but since I have no place to go / I resign myself to spending the night here." Osaka was a place in the mountains between Kyoto and Shiga Prefecture where there was a checking station for travelers. Perhaps the traveler now on his way through might never return. Similarly, Enshu felt that he would never again set eyes on a tea caddy like this one, and thus he chose the name Osaka.

From the Momoyama period through the early years of the Edo period, many handicraft works of art representative of the interval from the middle to the end of the Ming dynasty were brought over to Japan from China. Enshu made skillful use of such works, initiating a new "tea of Chinese wares," although it was not characterized by the severe rules of the Higashiyama period. The Chinese-style openwork tea-utensil stand shown in Figures 97 and 197 was made to Enshu's taste and has an air wholly in keeping with him. The water jar displayed on the stand is a product of the Takatori kiln in Kyushu, one of Enshu's Seven Kilns, as they were called, and it, too, was made to his taste.

The wares known as Old Sometsuke and produced in the late Ming dynasty during the 1620s were imported to Japan in vast quantities. Among them were many made to the taste of tea men, and the water jar with a design of grapevines and a trellis (Fig. 96) is representative of the Old Sometsuke wares designed for use as tea utensils. Such wares came into use from the time of Enshu, and in Yamashina Doan's *Kaiki* frequent mention is made of Old Sometsuke plates and bowls (Fig. 194).

The calligraphy of Fujiwara Teika was held in high esteem from the Momoyama period through the early Edo period. A renowned example of his work was the set of poem cards known as the *Ogura Shikishi* (Fig. 98), and both Hideyoshi and Ieyasu, in turn, had it in their possession. Also said to have been owned by Ieyasu is the *shikishi* on which Teika had inscribed a poem by Ise no Tayu, one of the Thirty-six Famous Poets in the mid-Heian period: "The cherry trees / that formerly filled the old capital, Nara, / with the glory of their double blossoms / today bloom in splendor / here at the court of the Heian capital." This poem, a eulogy of the emperor, symbolized by the cherry blossoms, was included in the *Shika Waka-shu* (Collection of Verbal Flowers), compiled in 1144.

Ninsei's decorated pottery was produced in the vicinity of the Ninna-ji temple at Omuro, Kyoto, and at the time was known as Omuro ware. As we have already seen, Ninsei's tea wares owed much to the guidance of Kanamori Sowa, to the extent that his work may be said to represent Sowa's taste. The incense burner in the shape of a pheasant (Fig. 101) is held to be the most outstanding of these works. The proud figure of the male pheasant is life-size, and the intent of the design achieves perfect expression. It is not clear whether or not this particular work was in keeping with Sowa's taste, but it is a masterpiece that displays Ninsei's ability to perfection.

From the closing years of the seventeenth century to about the 1730s, the culture of the merchants saw its full flowering, and their peculiar love of tea utensils reached its highest level of expression. It was at this time that the brothers Korin and Kenzan made their appearance and exhibited a rich decorative art in their paintings and pottery. The *Azaleas and Running Water* (Fig. 104) is a remarkable work that vividly illustrates the elegance of Korin.

Konoike Do-oku is a figure that stands for the merchants' taste for *meibutsu*, and his great wealth enabled him to collect many *meibutsu* masterpieces. The fact that he owned many *kinrande*, or gold-painted porcelains, made during the sixteenth century, in the middle years of Ming, is a point of interest in that it reflects to what extent his taste was that of a merchant. Others, too, like Konoe Yoraku-in, with whom he was close friends, combined the *kinrande* or Old Sometsuke extensively with Teika's calligraphy (Fig. 156) and displayed a tea style that fitted well with the culture of early-eighteenth-century Japan.

TITLES IN THE SERIES

Although the individual books in the series are designed as self-contained units, so that readers may choose subjects according to their personal interests, the series itself constitutes a full survey of Japanese art and is therefore a reference work of great value. The following titles are listed in the same order, roughly chronological, as those of the original Japanese versions, with the addition of a cultural appreciation (Vol. 30) and the index volume.

The "weathermark" identifies this book as a production of John Weatherhill, Inc., publishers of fine books on Asia and the Pacific. Supervising editor: Ralph Friedrich. Book design and typography: Meredith Weatherby. Layout of illustrations: Sigrid Nikovskis. Production supervisor: Yutaka Shimoji. Composition: General Printing Co., Yokohama. Color-plate engraving and printing: Hanshichi Photoprinting Co., Tokyo. Gravure-plate engraving and printing: Inshokan Printing Co., Tokyo. Monochrome letterpress platemaking and printing and text printing: Toyo Printing Co., Tokyo. Binding: Makoto Binderies, Tokyo. The typeface used is Monotype Baskerville, with hand-set Optima for display.